EXILES IN EDEN

EXILES
IN EDEN

Life Among the Ruins of
Florida's Great Recession

Paul Reyes

135810

HENRY HOLT AND COMPANY   NEW YORK

Henry Holt and Company, LLC
Publishers since 1866
175 Fifth Avenue
New York, New York 10010
www.henryholt.com

Henry Holt® and ⓗ® are registered trademarks of
Henry Holt and Company, LLC.

Distributed in Canada by H. B. Fenn and Company Ltd.

Portions of this book have appeared in *Harper's Magazine*,
The Oxford American, and *The Virginia Quarterly Review*.

"Root Cellar," copyright 1943 by Modern Poetry Association, Inc., from *Collected
Poems of Theodore Roethke*, by Theodore Roethke. Used by permission of Doubleday,
a division of Random House, Inc.

Library of Congress Cataloging-in-Publication Data

Reyes, Paul.
    Exiles in Eden : life among the ruins of Florida's great recession /
by Paul Reyes.
        p. cm.
    ISBN 978-0-8050-9123-6
    1. Subprime mortgage loans—Florida.   2. Foreclosure—Florida.
3. Global Financial Crisis, 2008–2009.   I. Title.
    HG2040.5.U6F616 2010
    330.9759'064—dc22   2010005738

Henry Holt books are available for special promotions and
premiums. For details contact: Director, Special Markets.

First Edition 2010

Designed by Kelly S. Too

Printed in the United States of America
1 3 5 7 9 10 8 6 4 2

For Ellen

Nothing would give up life:
Even the dirt kept breathing a small breath.

—Theodore Roethke, "Root Cellar"

Think different than others. Think outside the box. Turn impossible to possible. But you will benefit. Remember not everyone has the same ideas as you do. They don't see the potential as you do.

—Notes scribbled in Dean Graziosi's
Real Estate Millions: Personal Secrets, found in a foreclosed
double-wide trailer in Zephyrhills, Florida, February 2009

CONTENTS

SPRING:
THE ROUT

———

W hen I ask my father what he remembers about the first houses he trashed out—a phrase we use to describe the process of entering a home that has been foreclosed upon by the bank, and which the bank would like to sell, and hauling all of what the dispossessed owner has left behind to the nearest dump, then returning to clean the place by spraying every corner and wiping every inch of glass, deleting every fingerprint, scrubbing the boot marks off the linoleum, bleaching the cruddy toilets, sweeping up the hair and sand and dust, steaming the stains out of the carpet (or, if the carpet is unsalvageably rancid, tearing it out), and eventually, thereby, erasing all traces of whoever lived there, dispensing with both their physical presence and the ugly aura of eviction—he says he doesn't remember much. It was too many years ago, for one thing, well before I started working for him. And since then he has trashed out so much bizarre flotsam, under such strange circumstances, that his memories of those first few houses have faded.

None of the stories my father shares about this work—and

certainly none that I can tell—are uplifting. Sure, there are comedies and tragicomedies, and some plots are shot through with an absurdity that seems indigenous to Florida, where this began for us. But overall the circumstances remain bleakly fixed: Every foreclosed house, empty or not, clean or crumbling, feels lost, no matter the neighborhood or amenities, no matter the waterfront view. Some houses are left spotless, others in a wretched degradation, and the varieties are shared among the rich and poor, the elderly and the upwardly mobile. Some houses are lost before ever being lived in; others, abandoned long ago, provide shelter for addicts, bums, whores, snakes, strays, and low fungal kingdoms that fan out in the darkness, kick-started, maybe, by a cat turd or bowl of leftovers.

The junk left behind has fascinated me since I began working foreclosures with my father years ago—during holidays, or between jobs, boomeranging between Tampa and wherever I ended up next—tagging along with his regular crew, a pair of Puerto Rican laborers who start the day at six and call it at three. I have always been the crew's weak link, both because I flinch in places that, after months of abandonment, have become so gloriously foul, and because I can't help but read a narrative in what has been discarded—an impulse that evolved into a purpose, just as the trash-out itself evolved from a job that paid when writing didn't into a way of examining a national crisis up close. So I've picked and gleaned, sweating nearly every item we've thrown away, creeping among the gadgets and notes and utility bills and photographs in order to decipher who lived there and how they lost it, a life partially revealed by stuff marinating in a fetid stillness. It is a guilt-ridden literary forensics, because to confront the junk is to confront the individuality being purged from a place. My father was never all that interested in this particular angle. He likes to keep things simple: He gets an address, the crew goes to work. Now and then I join them, but I've never been much good at keeping up.

Foreclosures are our family business, but a line of work my father arrived at after some professional meandering. José Miguel Reyes met and married my mother, Franny Picón Blanco, in Philadelphia in 1969. He was twenty-two, a Cuban refugee who'd spent his teenage years in the camps of Miami, and who, after moving north, found work running errands for the draftsmen at United Engineers. My mother, a Colombian girl, had arrived in time to attend high school in the States, and was diligent enough to grind her way toward a diploma while still getting her American bearings (math was easy, she says; *Othello*, not so much).

After marriage, and having me, my parents etched a constellation of hometowns up and down the East Coast, landing in Florida in 1984. After starting his own small construction company, and losing it, and after a relatively diplomatic divorce from my mother and a brief midlife crisis, my father married again, to a real estate agent this time. They began dabbling in houses—repairing them, restoring the historic ones, flipping most for a modest profit. His second wife, Mena, had been selling foreclosures for a while. Now, when it came time to clean a foreclosure out and fix it up, a job hardly anyone else wanted, my father was more than willing.

This turned out to be steady, predictable work, tucked in the margins of an otherwise healthy housing market. In the early 1990s, when my father and Mena began working together, foreclosures were, for the most part, quiet aberrations in real estate, the result of extremes: someone sick and uninsured, leveraging a home to cover bills; some couple spiraling through divorce, with neither one willing to pay the mortgage on a house neither wanted; gamblers who'd overextended themselves; addicts who'd finally unraveled. Among them all, the most common were the sick and brokenhearted. "Back then," my father says, "what you saw the most were X-rays on the floor, medical records here and there, divorce papers. You didn't see so many notices from banks. Back then, it was a combination of getting into debt and losing a job, getting into debt and going through a divorce, getting into debt and having medical problems. Not just getting into debt."

By and large, these were hidden tragedies. But as strange and unpleasant as this business was, it was also a way for a real estate agent to stretch out a little, to make a living in a less crowded field. By the mid '90s, agents were as ubiquitous as tourists, with would-be landlords trailing them. One degree separated you, it seemed, from someone in real estate—and in Florida, as in generations past, real estate embraced all comers.

The temptation, of course, was based on housing's reputation as a sound investment. The 5 percent rule—that a home's value increased by about as much every year—guided most buyers' expectations, because for the better part of a century the rule held true. And while the housing market endured booms and busts and bubbles over the decades, the value of a home generally crept ever upward, so that by the end of the century the longstanding faith in a home as a sound investment was tightly thatched together with the dream it was meant to inspire. Nostalgia and pragmatism, pride and profit. By and large, the dream paid.

But by the early 2000s, the political and economic forces that helped build this wealth had fallen into a dangerous groove. As activists, legislators, and presidents pushed for greater expansion in homeownership, mortgages—which for years had been bundled, spliced, and sold several times over as a tradable Wall

Street commodity—evolved from a dull investment into a hot product. It wasn't just political pressure that made the mortgage-backed security so popular; in the early 2000s, the global economic landscape was such that the mortgage-backed security became comparatively profitable to other investments. What's more, deregulation had widened the field of players and expanded the list of what they were allowed to do. Thus, with deregulation, politicians had provided the blessing, blending the mandate of homeownership with the free-market incentive to provide it. As investors demanded more mortgages to trade, lenders took greater risks in providing them. Soon enough, the subprime loan (one issued to a high-risk borrower) became a dangerously ubiquitous chit, and its varieties speak to the frenzy that evolved: Stated Income Verified Assets, Stated Income Stated Assets, No Income Verified Assets, No Income No Assets (aka "Liar Loans"). Borrowers were lured with adjustable payments, deferred payments, interest rates that were harmless at first, but which doubled or tripled after a handful of years. Some homeowners borrowed 110 percent of the value of a house; others borrowed ten times what they made in a year. Easy money after just a few questions, nothing too invasive. And if a borrower's economic truth didn't bear out, the commission was all the motivation a broker needed to fudge the math. Maids became landlords. Condominiums became a kind of currency. In some cases, even the dead qualified for a loan.

Homeownership became a self-perpetuating addiction: As more people qualified to own a home, more people wanted one, and as the demand for homes increased, so did the price. By 2004, the 5 percent rule had become obsolete, and the faith in homeownership warped into hysteria, with home prices in cities across the country increasing by as much as 30 percent a year.

By the middle of the decade, at the housing bubble's peak, the rise in home values had eclipsed all booms dating back a century and then some. Not even the postwar boom could touch it. And with this explosion in value, homes were leveraged to the hilt, for reasons both intelligent and frivolous—a new kitchen, a vacation, other debts.

In this market, reckless loans and poor decisions had few consequences. The market was hot enough that the high-interest-rate traps waiting to reset after two or five years seemed like empty threats, since a home could be refinanced or sold before the trap sprung. The same held true for homeowners who fell behind in payments. And if a bank did eventually repossess a home, they could usually sell it for more than the loan itself. So foreclosures didn't linger. For every home lost, odds were that a buyer—new parents looking for a first home, an investor looking for a rental—could be found in a matter of weeks.

Then, in late 2005, the market crested. Buyers paused. Building slowed. And the break in momentum was just enough to reveal how precarious all that wealth had been, since the housing market slowed only briefly before collapsing altogether. *Upside down* and *underwater*—owing more on a home than the home is actually worth: Once stigmatic phrases, these became contagious in 2007. The convoluted, spring-loaded mortgages and home-equity loans taken out in the early 2000s had reset. Rates skyrocketed. Homeowners who'd borrowed so heavily against a phantom value now found themselves trapped in houses worth less and less every day. Even after foreclosure, the prices kept dropping, and as the price of a foreclosure dropped, so did the value of the houses around it, a viral depreciation that led, in some cases, to entire blocks of families owing more on their mortgages than the homes could be sold for. To quantify it: In a little under two years, between the peak of Tampa's housing market, in July 2006, to the spring of 2008, the value of homes in the Bay Area's counties (Hillsborough, Pinellas, Hernando, Pasco) dropped by over 26 percent, reflecting a panic nearly equal to the pace at which prices had reached their summer peak. The hysteria that had inflated Florida's real estate bubble was simply a primer for the collapse that followed. The 5 percent rule had been reversed with a vengeance.

By the spring of 2008, when I returned home to work and write about the crisis, buyers had long since disappeared, and houses by the thousands—both new and old—sat empty, beginning their slow corrosion. The crowds that once camped outside subdivision gates, hoping to snatch a prime lot, had evaporated, and the subdivisions were devouring their own value: Homes built in 2006 had been repossessed within a year and were now selling for half as much as surrounding homes, finished just that summer. Some homeowners, exasperated, were simply walking away from their debt, mailing the keys to the bank. Others barricaded themselves in and waited.

And the foreclosures kept coming. What had been a rotation of about fifteen houses to inspect on my father's list had swelled to eighty, and hovered there, no matter how many were fixed up and sold again. If Mena couldn't move a foreclosure, it was assigned to another agent, or was tossed into one of the massive auctions that blared through town every season like a circus. Of course, champions of the free market, my father among them, argued that the market would, in due time, and in typically robust fashion, correct itself. For the rest of us the question had become, *At what cost?* What amount of carnage would be required?

And while the Treasury weighed its billion-dollar pledges to the institutions that had engineered the biggest economic collapse since the Great Depression, the statistical damage on the ground was giving that comparison some weight: Between the time Florida's housing market began to cool off in 2005 and my arrival there in the spring, the rate of homes being lost had quadrupled, to more than 35,000 per month, nearly 5,000 of which were in cities within my father's working radius—Tampa, St. Petersburg, Clearwater. The collapse was surreal in its proportion, biblical in its egalitarian reach, like an economic cleansing fire.

Which meant that all spring, we were flush with work.

E very homecoming, the weather is a surprise. Barreling down I-95 or I-75, or slipping through the panhandle on I-10, shooting through the northern counties, right around Gaines-ville, in a riot of oaks and palms and hills and swamp, a lush air folds shut against the mainland, as if the life ahead—a longer daylight, a funky dampness—is exclusive to those leaving the bulk of America behind them. Florida is a mistress state of moguls, few arts to speak of; rather, the weather is the culture. And while it is an extension of the continent, it isn't quite of a piece with it. Crossing Alachua County, just below the thirtieth par-allel, water begins to take over.

Flying into Tampa International, the weather is just as obvi-ous: It greets you first. In winter, at thirty thousand feet, the pilot's forecast—seventy-three degrees, a mild humidity—elicits coos from the cabin; in the spring and summer, mostly silence. What makes a homecoming by flight so surprisingly strange, each time, is that landing at Tampa International is nostalgic at all. But it is, without fail—a pleasant and suddenly familiar shock as I cross the open space between the fusilage and walk-way, where the outside air sneaks in, having barely thanked the flight attendant before inhaling the sharp cocktail of jet fuel and sea breeze, factory and ocean, and in that instant recalling the Florida I grew up with, exhumed from several layers deep inside the skin.

On a drizzly March afternoon just a couple of weeks before Easter, I got my fix. The air at Tampa International was thick and close and laced with salt from the Gulf. The tram sped us from the gate to the terminal, and there I found my father wait-ing, grinning, the white lamps high above shining against his head where his hair had receded, and off his cheeks, too (his mother's cheeks, which I inherited). His balding head betrayed his age; his cheeks kept him boyish. He looked slightly thinner than he was at Christmas, still heavy, but more slope-shouldered, his short-sleeved dress shirt long in the sleeves and loose.

He gave me a subtle hug and a slap on the back of the head with his folded newspaper. He'd been absorbing headlines lately: CASTRO QUITS ONE ROLE, BUT MAY NOT BE DONE YET; FORECLO-SURES PROMPT CITIES TO PLEA FOR U.S. AID. His profession and fatherland were at a crossroads. What's more, Venezuela's Hugo Chávez had sent troops to the Colombian border the day before, as a countermove to Colombia's raid of a FARC camp on the Ecuadoran side (such was Chávez's trigger-happy nature). My father had married two Colombians, both my mother and Mena, which meant that between Christmas and spring, history seemed to be folding together. Housing, Cuba, Colombia: a trifecta of relevance.

As for the hug and slap on the head, I expected as much. My father has always asserted himself playfully through such ges-tures. Slaps on the head, gentle chiding, a little nitpicking now and then on my appearance—all goofy reminders of the natural family order. But then down at the baggage claim, he grabbed my satchel and deferred the heavier bags to me, and I remembered: His back had become unpredictable a few years ago— after a big sneeze, of all things. This was a new weakness, following a tricky heart (his mother's cheeks, his father's heart). So I carried the heavy luggage, and of course his pride pricked at him. In the elevator, after gently deflecting my excitement about the news from Cuba, he looked at me and said, with no small dose of disapproval, "You need a haircut."

Out on the highway, the traffic poured from the airport and split along overpasses, blending with thicker tendrils of more traffic that flowed out toward the suburbs and sprawl. We headed east on an errand: a foreclosure on Hillsborough Lane. Whoever lived in the house had ignored the first notice my father posted, prompting a second notice, same as the first, to call Mena. Once a house is foreclosed upon, Mena, at the bank's request, will prepare it to be placed back on the market. If the house is occupied, she can sometimes negotiate a less painful exit, through a cash-for-keys exchange. If the owner refuses, the bank sends the sheriff, an expert messenger of bad news and ultimatums.

My father had already visited this house once before, to see whether it was occupied. A rottweiler in the front yard was a pretty good clue, and so he left the first notice in the mailbox, on the prudent side of a chain-link fence. My father knew nothing about the occupant. He almost never does at first. He's given an address and a name, and in this case he didn't even have the name. All he had was the rottweiler. "Bad," he said. "Black."

"All rottweilers are black," I said.

"Well, this one was *black*."

We took the Waters Avenue exit off the freeway and dipped down onto the street, rolling past the Derby Lane dog track (DOGS, PONIES, POKER!), past the All Nations Outreach Center, past a meat market, past black men in white T's weaving on bikes too small for their legs to pedal seated, past black girls in bathing suits ambling on the sidewalk, headed for the public pool, or just dressed for the heat, ignoring the rain that had begun to fall. We were in Sulphur Springs, one of Tampa's early suburbs, famous in the 1920s as a spring-fed sanctuary from the city, a ghetto now. "Suffer Springs," we called it. Nebraska Avenue cut through the heart of it, close to the "miraculous waters" of the river and water tower, now flanked by a hodgepodge of car dealerships and carpet warehouses and diners, and billboards promising loans and mortgages to practically anyone with the power to call. The only architectural freshness to the neighborhood was in the Section 8 homes, relatively new and recently painted, bright among the dilapidated early-century bungalows. Passing the Section 8's we could see a cluster of squad cars and cops surrounding a ravaged-looking dude splayed across a bench in front of an open-air Laundromat. You had a good angle on the action from the porches of those Section 8's.

At Hillsborough Lane we turned and coasted until we passed the house, then squeaked to a stop. We sat still, the truck idling quietly, and with the drizzle against the windshield the stillness swelled a little. I looked at the houses surrounding this one: Some neighbors were barely keeping it together; other houses teetered further toward squalor. The block was a mash of hasty, low architecture, single-story, pale cinder-block jobs squatting under live oaks sagging with Spanish moss. In front of the house on our list stood a four-by-four post, about seven feet tall, with a pair of digital-satellite dishes screwed to the top. Next to it, the mailbox: orange, plastic, and empty.

It was quiet. The dog was missing. The chain-link gate was wide open. The yard was a psoriatic patchwork of grass and gray sand. Judging by the size of the plywood doghouse, the rottweiler was as big as Dad described. The yard reflected its temperament: blown-out pits within the radius of a long chain anchored by an enormous dumbbell half-buried in the sand. Lizards—thick and deep-black, masculine, and, after a childhood in Florida, nostalgically repulsive to me—scuttled along the top of the fence.

The rain thickened. The wipers dragged slowly back and forth. A FOR SALE sign leaned toward the street.

"That wasn't there a couple of days ago," my father said, and *humphed.* "He can say he wants to sell it all he wants to, he's not going to cover the debt."

My father pulled a notice from between the driver's seat and the armrest. Every notice he posts is the same: a black-and-white photocopy of Mena's business card with instructions to contact her. In the top-right corner of the card was her portrait—smiling, professionally shot, the light softened a little, a popular head shot among real estate agents. My father laid the paper flat on his briefcase and began scribbling the simple instructions in pencil, in the penmanship he'd learned as a draftsman and which I've always admired for its precision but have never been able to imitate exactly—capital, architectural letters, perfectly straight, the joints of each letter bolted together, the words aligned as if written along a phantom ruler, impossible to misread: PLEASE CALL MENA. WE ARE OFFERING CASH FOR KEYS. With the bank's approval, Mena was prepared to offer whoever was inside cash for keys to the house (in this case, five hundred dollars), provided it was cleaned out first—a small amelioration, but cash nonetheless.

Normally, he would have taped the notice to the door and ducked out. But it was raining, and the rottweiler, though out of sight, might still have been napping around back, and so my father merely slipped out of the truck, shoved the notice into the mailbox, then slipped back in.

"I'm surprised you haven't been shot," I said.

"It's always on my mind," he said, and began scribbling down the FOR SALE sign's phone number. He slid the gearshift into drive and looked around, disappointed. That mythical black motherfucker of a dog . . . he wanted me to see it for myself.

Early the next morning, setting out in a bruise-colored light, we lurched for a painfully slow mile behind a school bus blinking to a stop every twenty yards or so, nearly the whole distance to the day's first inspection, a single-story 2/2 (two bedrooms, two baths) on Centennial Court, one of dozens of short cul-de-sacs set off a winding main road. It was a dense neighborhood, remarkable only for its anonymity, built in the postwar boom but whose homes didn't seem to embody the American dream as prescribed. At best, these were starter kits to the dream, their privacy fences tagged with graffiti, their roofs sprouting satellite dishes, often two at a time—a sign, my father said, that the family inside was Hispanic, since one dish would be for American television, a second for Spanish-language channels.

We pulled up to the 2/2, jimmied the front-door lock, stepped inside, and took a look around. Dad guessed the owners must have been Hispanic, since nearly every square inch of floor was covered with white tile, a common, simple cooling system. I doubted it, since tile floors were popular in rentals, a cheap and easy way to clean up after messy tenants. But then, in the corner of the backyard, another clue: a makeshift *caja china*, a box in which a pig is sealed and slowly roasted under coals piled atop the lid, a fixture of the Cuban or Puerto Rican yard. It was little more than a tub for rainwater now, swarming with ants that had carried off the pig's drippings but still searched for more.

The house held a strange loot: pleather couch, a weightlifting set, empty liquor bottles. The garage had been halfway converted into a bedroom, with a mattress wedged under a clothes rack. All over were signs of a messy exodus, with half a dozen garbage bags sitting full but untied like the last abandoned task. I dug into the bags: Every single one was crammed with toys, mostly stuffed animals and dolls.

"Here," Dad said as he kicked a headlight casing. "It's a motorcycle . . . thing."

I picked up a motorcycle helmet, looked into its visor a moment, then tossed it aside.

In the rest of the junk, a vague story came together: Sindy lived with Robert, but they didn't share a last name. Perhaps she was a stepdaughter, or a roommate, because in the back bedroom, under stripes of veloured sunlight, SINDY & CHRI$ was stenciled on the wall in black, with a devil's tail whipping underneath. So Sindy (twenty-five, judging by a birthday card) belonged to Chris, but other than the stenciled dedication there wasn't a trace of him. Perhaps Robert had something to do with it, perhaps he was a bit overprotective. But it was hard to say.

One thing was certain: Someone had a brave taste in booze. The bottles scattered throughout the tiny kitchen—Seagram's, Crown Royal, Hine, Hennessy, Bacardi, Holland Vodka (in a bong-shaped bottle), and Brugal rum—suggested a slovenly habit of keeping empties, or a blowout near the end. The way the pad-ded dining chairs were angled against the window-side table, with the bottles knocked over, lent some credence to the rager theory, in which Sindy and Robert and whoever else—bags full in the next room, their sofa too heavy to carry, the sheriff on his way—drank up their courage, kicked aside a box or two, and headed out into an unpredictable future.

Between addresses, we made a quick stop at the Cuban *panadería*, a ritual of my visits home. We hovered over the cartoonishly bright pastries until called upon, ordered a couple of *cafés con leche* and, while waiting, admired the fried stuff—*chicharrón*, *jamón croquetas*, *papa rellena*, all bronze and garish and sultry under the heat lamp. Salsa music played softly above us. The doorbell dinged. The small crowd swelled and ebbed with regu-lars dedicated to a brave motherland diet. The tiny room was thick with the odors of hot oil and coffee and sugar and warm bread. And sure, pork rinds for breakfast might mean fewer days in the long run, but they added a weird vigor to the morning. If anything, the grease is sentimental.

We took turns rummaging through the bag on the way to the next house, passing through Odessa's dense stretches of cypress and oak, one of the last rural strongholds this close to Tampa. We were headed for Holiday Park, a good forty minutes away. The rate of expansion for foreclosures, and Mena's will-ingness to accept them, meant that my father's work radius had expanded, too. Logging a hundred miles a day had become com-mon, leaving plenty of time for window gazing and small talk.

We lit on the subject of breaking into a house. My father's

preferred method, which he'd used on Centennial, was to slide a flathead screwdriver between door and frame, then leverage the cylinder out of the lock as he twisted the doorknob with a clamp wrench. "You're bending the insides," he said. "All you need is about a quarter of an inch. It's got a shaft, and the shaft is connected to the cylinder, so if you pull it back enough—"

"What did you do before that?"

"Bang it with a hammer. But that messed up the door. This is more surgical. And if it fails, you use a drill and open holes in it so you can get to it. Drill directly into the deadbolt. Those things are cheap, the deadbolts. Once you open three or four holes, it falls apart."

"So it's that easy to break into a house?"

"Oh, yeah," he said. "We've never failed to get into a house. There is always a way."

Out the window, across acres of cleared land, I could see a subdivision frozen in an early phase of construction. A handful of pastel-colored nouveau-Victorian townhouses stood quiet, surrounded by empty, readied lots, then just dirt that faded into the scrub of a cleared field. There was no activity whatsoever near the beginnings of that neighborhood—no earthmovers, no foremen, not even a pickup truck darting across a street. Just a ghost town starting at two hundred dollars a square foot. Nearer to us, along the shoulder of the road, the power company was laying lines for the expansion of utilities, the county undeterred in its optimistic vision for growth.

"If not," my father said, "you take the sliding doors, lift them up off the track, and they come out."

I didn't get it.

"Well, typically, those doors, people never adjust them, so they settle, to a point where there's enough room on top so that you can lift them higher than the track and pull them out. People use them for years without adjusting them. At the bottom, that little wheel can be adjusted up and down. Over time, it wears down. That's all you need."

The truck's GPS device guided us to our next job, a house on Anaheim Avenue, but couldn't tell us where the house was exactly. Three lawns down, though, we saw it: a pair of white wicker chairs, one crushed, leaning against the trunk of a bedraggled live oak, as if pitched there by a wind. A few feet away, iron patio chairs lay facedown like drunks passed out on the lawn. The house was a mid-century ranch, maybe a little more recent, with tall windows stretching between the bushes and the eaves.

We got out. The lawn was carpeted with the live oak's brittle, mustard-colored leaves—months of untended shedding, if not a year's worth. An elderly couple walked past and stared, and I waved. The breeze picked up, the air was lush. Nimbus clouds sauntered high behind the roof. We walked around to the back of the house, past a futon frame cradling a pile of branches, toward a picket fence, where we crossed into a small yard. A bird fountain leaned at the fence's edge. A pond opened up behind it, with other houses flanking the far bank. My father walked up to the screen door of the sunroom. He pressed his face against the glass and *humphed*. "I know I can get into this one," he said.

Circling back around, we checked the front door—locked— and peeked through the tall front windows into the living room. The curtains were missing. In the middle of the living room, on the carpet, sat an electric stove and a wicker shelf for a menagerie, toppled on its side.

"You sure this is unoccupied?" I said.

"Mena thinks it is," he said.

A small yellow notice taped to the window, stuck there by an agent of Fidelity Information Services, confirmed that the house was vacant. The window screen leaned on the ground, and we figured this must have been how Fidelity's agent had slipped in. I was busy reading the rest of the notice as my father bent down and yanked the window open, the springs cracking—*The mortgage holder has the right and duty to protect this property accordingly. It is likely that the mortgage holder will have the property . . .* —and let the window slam shut.

"See," Dad said, muted behind the glass. "There is *always* a way."

Inside, surrounded by half-full boxes, I began scribbling down a partial inventory:

> 1 wicker throne
> 1 walkie-talkie
> The White Album
> Masterplots (6 volumes)
> 15 pairs of women's shoes
> Mother's Day card, signed, "Love, Us"
> Glasses, one pair

The owner's name was Sue, a fact gleaned from the pile of bills and letters left on the bedroom floor. The paper trail told that she had inherited money from a will, apparently, then spent it, and was collecting Social Security by the time she lost the house. She'd scribbled epigrams and lyrics on index cards and coupons: "Words express both the best & worse of life. Let the words you choose express the life you wont to live"—"Send me a man that Reads"—"She walked across his heart like it was Texas"—"He was on the morning side of the mountain, She was on the twilight side of the hill."

She struggled with work. Birthday and Mother's Day cards and letters included encouragements and best wishes in finding jobs, be it in 1999 or 2002. One birthday card had a basset hound on the cover, a hint that she owned one. In fact, she owned two— Hanzel and Gretel—whose vet bills were in the pile, and against whom an injunction had been filed in court, for nuisance and trespassing. I couldn't find a picture of her or of anyone she knew. All the framed photographs that remained were of models in generic scenes, a publicity still from *Titanic*, and a stock photo of the Golden Gate Bridge.

I could hear my father in another room, taking pictures with a disposable camera, cranking to the next frame, clicking. I followed the sound to the pine-paneled sunroom, through the windows of which I could see an egret alight on the edge of the pond. Bad guess—my father was elsewhere—but in this room was stacked a set of boxes that suggested Sue was an ambitious reader with eclectic tastes: Huxley's *Brave New World*, several Sidney Sheldon titles, Danielle Steel, Bartlett's *Familiar Quotations*, a thesaurus, *The Irritable Bowel Syndrome Gastrointestinal Solutions Handbook*, Hemingway, a waterlogged *Don Quixote*, Salinger, I. F. Stone's *The War Years*, *Reader's Digest*, *The 9 Steps to Financial Freedom*, *Love Handles for the Romantically Impaired*. Books on thinking positively, on self-hypnosis, on UFOs, on Darwinism. I found copies of *Dog Fancy* magazine and a long-outdated issue of *The Best and Worst Makeovers Ever*. There were boxes stuffed with monographs on Dalí, Toulouse-Lautrec, Picasso; books on Art Nouveau, on the Impressionists, on the painters of Montmartre. A stack of travel sections from the local newspaper, and an article on "Five Myths about Reagan."

I went to the shed out back and found more books—in boxes, lined up on a makeshift shelf, stacked in a pile among Christmas gift wrapping, lodged against picture frames swaddled in blankets. It was a shrine of sorts. Here, apparently, was everything that pertained to a late husband, Herb, whose effects had been stored long enough to dissolve in the Florida heat. Shelby Foote's Civil War trilogy rotted next to the Harvard Classics; millipedes chewed through John Jakes. The humidity had devoured Herb's yearbooks. His memory seemed to have been entombed in this shed for years and never visited. Even the stove had made it closer to an exit than Herb had.

My father called Mena to fill her in. One bedroom, unoccupied, with a two-car garage and central heat and air. The pond out back was a plus.

Hector, bronze and balding, his thick waist wrapped in a weightlifting belt, is the bullish half of my father's two-man crew. He stands a broad five feet eight, with forearms thick as hams that seem divinely built for ripping things apart. He moved from Puerto Rico more than twenty years ago and began working for my father soon after. English still eludes Hector, and only when he attempts it does he reveal a shyness. When he speaks his native Spanish, he spouts it with a drill sergeant's urgency, a rabid muttering loaded with idiom, nearly unintelligible. Even my father shrugs at most of what Hector says, or asks him to repeat it, slowly. Hector is also furiously born-again; there is no telling what topic will trigger one of his irritable calls to Christ.

Ismael, also Puerto Rican, is Hector's Sancho Panza. He is in his early seventies, but is so small and fumbling that, with Hector, at least, he fails to win the respect due the elderly. Hector often barks at him, or corrects him, or berates him when he's klutzy. Ismael tends to stay quiet in Hector's presence, except when the insult is too painful to endure, and then he snaps back at him. He despises Hector for his discourtesy, but he has been working with him for fifteen years now, and they have become grudgingly inseparable, like a marriage or a bitter vaudeville act. And they are mule-like in their constancy and fearlessness when it comes to digging through repugnant places.

Three in the truck, tiny Ismael in the middle, we were on our way to Sue's house to trash it out. Religious folk music blasted out of the speakers—Hector's favorite group: Spanish, melodic, and sweet, a family of singers, children and all. I asked him what he thought the difference was between the job now and in years past. Now, he said, everyone was mixed up in it, every race and every class. Now, he shouted, in Spanish and with an evangelical urgency, "It's much more than you think. *¡Son de todo! Todo, todo!*"

"All mix," Ismael muttered.

"You know why so many people are losing their houses?" Hector asked. "Yeah, sure, people lose their jobs, but the majority—thousands! hundreds of thousands!—they lost their homes because the people at the bank, many of them, are wicked! They don't tell you that the interest rates are going to go up. They just make you sign the papers. They cheat you!"

Ismael, inspired, blurted out: "You need to think about your resources, whether you have the means or not to pay for a house. That's why the Bible says, 'For which one of you, when he wants to build a tower, does not first sit down and calculate—'"

Hector cut him off: "No, that's different, that's not what I'm talking about."

"It's the same thing."

"No, totally different."

"Buy only what you—"

"We're talking about something else."

They fell silent. We drove for a while listening to the absurdly tiny voices of what sounded like abnormally tiny children, off-key, with a contrapuntal bass line rolling over classical guitar.

Hector picked up a lost thread, left a few miles back when I asked if he'd seen the Jones-Trinidad fight. Part of the ritual with Hector was to talk about boxing, his passion, but a sport he said he'd given up watching because of the violence it encour-aged, technically a sin. So he didn't see the fight, he said. "But I heard Tito got beat up. What was he thinking? He already lost to Jones in a lower weight class. What did he think was going to happen at a heavier one! He should've fought a rematch with De La Hoya." Whether he'd seen it or not, he knew every punch of every round.

I wondered if he had ever seen mixed martial arts on televi-sion, what he and Ismael called "boxeo-karate."

"That stuff is awful," Hector said. "They don't even use gloves! This one guy, I saw it, he tried to tap out and the other guy didn't see him and kept punching him and the guy died." He paused. "I like wrestling," he said, "'cause it's fixed. A guy can get hit in the head ten times on Friday, and on Saturday get hit again another ten times. In wrestling they maybe get a knee injury or break their collarbone, but other than that, it's not that dangerous."

"The best at boxeo-karate is Chuck Norris," Ismael said.

"*Now* he is," Hector corrected him. "Before, it was Bruce Lee. But they killed him. People can say what they want, he was mur-dered."

"They murdered his son, too," Ismael said, darkening this conspiracy.

And the topics piled up, Hector holding forth with brim-stone vigor on the absurd distinction between apartments and condominiums, on the year's big fights, on the definition of "meat" at certain restaurants, and, since Easter was approaching, on his church's splendid reenactment of the Stations of the Cross. "Ninety-nine percent of people," he went on, "if you ask them, they say yes, I'm a Christian. And you then ask them, 'What does it mean to be Christian?' They don't know. To be a Christian isn't just going to church. It's much more than that." He hunched and glanced around. "What's the street we're looking for?"

"Humbolt," I said, and he jammed the brakes and hooked a left.

At Sue's house, Hector backed up to the garage door (he's masterful when it comes to maneuvering the truck and trailer in reverse, doing it with more speed than he should), I yanked the garage door open, and we went to work. We aired the house out, tackled different rooms. From the bedroom I could hear Hector reprimanding Ismael for misunderstanding some direction on where to put what. Paint cans went along the south wall of the garage; anything metal went in the yard; items for the church went on the opposite side of the trailer. Whenever Ismael saw me after some heated exchange ("Leave the paint there." "But you told me to move the paint—" "Leave it!"), he'd mutter something and roll his eyes, already frustrated. Fast, gloveless, and without much curiosity, the two of them loaded the first trailer in half an hour. For one cabinet too heavy to drag, Hector grabbed the sledgehammer and brought down devastation upon it, then tossed it on the pile, piece by piece.

"We throw away so much good stuff," he said, back inside. "You go to a flea market, what do you see? The same stuff we throw away, they're selling!"

He was, as usual, on a roll. But then, as I sat there trying to figure out the whys and hows of the stove in the middle of the living room, Hector appeared, shy all of a sudden. He nodded toward the front door, as if to suggest I go see what the matter was, and there in the driveway I saw a white-bearded man in an electric wheelchair, jerking back and forth. He must have wheeled up on Hector and started asking questions in English, Hector's weakness.

His name was John, and he'd been Sue's neighbor for years. He wore white socks, no shoes, and a baseball cap brandishing a phrase I couldn't make out but for something declarative about America. He'd moved here from Rochester long ago, he said ("good little city, just freeze your cayuns off"), and had been keeping an eye on Sue's house in the year since she'd left. He took drags off his cigarette with every sentence, and flicked the wheelchair's joystick with that same smoking hand. He seemed curious but not much impressed by us.

But what did he know about Sue? "She was eccentric," he said. "She'd do little crazy stuff. She'd be out here watering that tree—stupid things."

"They left a lot of stuff behind," I said.

"They took a lot with 'em."

A box of dishes crashed inside.

"She used to come over to my house all the time and visit," he said. "She had that home equity. She borrowed against the house, and the way houses went down, she owed more than what the house is worth."

Hector emerged with a box, tossed it in a high arc onto the trailer's pile.

"They took about five loads of a trailer this size," John said. "She had a lot of good antiques, but a lot of this here is junk. I'd check up to make sure nothing was happening to the house, but I don't think anybody's going to steal junk. Besides," he said, and twisted toward the neighborhood, "my son lives on the other side of me, my brother-in-law lives across the street, my brother lives in the house next door. My buddy lives over there. They all carry .357 Magnums all day, so it wouldn't be a good place to rob."

A single-prop buzzed low overhead. The wind picked up. Hector tossed the end of a rope over to where Ismael waited for it, to tie the junk down. The rope slapped Ismael on the head. "My face," he said, pronouncing it slowly; he liked to test his English in front of others.

"Well, we should get going," I said, and John nodded, then spun around and out of the way as we tied the junk down. We left several boxes of pewter goblets behind, tucked in a corner of the back patio so that Hector could recover them later, for the church.

The house locked, we eased back onto the street with a loaded pile, and after a quick stop at a hot-dog vendor in the parking lot of a defaulted store, we aimed for the dump—the Pasco County Solid Waste Resource Recovery Facility, which wasn't the closest facility, but the easiest. No sorting out the garbage, hardly any questions asked. What you spent in gas you saved in hassle. This was a preserve of waste, almost sylvan if you took care not to breathe. But the stench of rot reached at least a quarter mile out. "Smells like cake!" Hector shouted as we passed through the gate. "Coffee cake!"

We drove up a hill and into a hangar that housed the main incinerator. A mountain of garbage rose about four stories high along the east wall, out of a pit that sank another six or so stories down into the earth. A crane glided along the top of the wall, with a massive claw that swung from a cable. The claw would lower, clamp shut, and lift a dripping, car-sized pile up to and over the lip of the wall, where it would open and drop the pile down the other side, out of sight and into the fire.

A cheery inspector signaled us into the proper slot, then observed what we dragged from the trailer. We chatted. Across the hangar, the claw kept picking up and dumping garbage in the same spot, kneading the trash like a fist in dough. "To make it fluffy," the inspector said, because fluffy garbage burns better.

There, among the whines of reversing garbage trucks, the shriek and hiss of brakes, the groaning of horns, Sue's possessions slid down into a heap, got fluffed, and were carried over the wall to burn, dissolve, and compress, all traces of what she once prized dragged along the sludge and shoved over the edge into an ash pile so tidal in its proportions as to be barely comprehensible. Foreclosures, in their own way, regenerate: One family's loss can be another's first home. But this was the colossal deposit left behind, and it was growing by the cubic foot, by the ton.

Pulling out of the hangar, driving toward the landfill's exit, we could see the bulldozers perched high up on the trash bluff, where their drivers awaited orders to till another layer, to massage that Kilimanjaro of garbage, and where, if they looked away from the incinerator, they would have had a pretty good view of the city from whose ruin that mountain grew, and into whose streets we now descended to fetch the next load.

When we weren't dragging trash—splintered speakers, hula hoops, mildewed fur coats—onto the trailer, or from the trailer onto a larger pile at the dump, we drove. For hours. We visited nearly every landfill within a three-county radius, calculating the cost of gas to cover the distance against the hassle of sorting the trash ourselves.

With so many miles to cover, the truck became Hector's sweaty, Christ-soaked soapbox, and a kind of campfire tent, too, for weird yarns about what he and Ismael had seen during trash-outs.

"We went to one house," Hector said. "These people lived like cockroaches. They left everything, but nothing worked! Useless. The dogs had shit everywhere. In the laundry room, there was about three feet of clothing on the floor. And when we went into the garage? Same thing. It took us four days to clean that house, and I don't know how many trips to the dump!"

The squalor is a shock every time, each excavation a peek into a state of mind, like dismantling some diorama of dejection.

Each one of us at this job has been desperate, despondent, lazy, and otherwise lacking, but the scattered depravity of these vanquished homeowners remains humbling. They seem to lose a little of themselves. I've come across traces of vanished pets, their dried piles in almost every corner of the house and in between. Then there are the refrigerators, tombs of rot trapped for long enough that when we happen to open them, they release a florid wretchedness, an odor never entirely contained within the box, so that sometimes creatures have been drawn inside and, startled by the intrusion, spring out.

"¡Chacho!" Hector said. "We find snakes all the time. In refrigerators; snakes in luggage. One time we even found the skin of a—what do you call it—a python!"

Snakes and dog shit, curd and bees. Depressing as the rancid houses are, though, their desolation is rivaled by that of the houses left in a state of creepy tidiness. The house on Vanderbilt Drive was one such job, in a subdivision called Ashley Lakes: a six-bedroom, four-bathroom box with a second-story view of other roofs, a house new enough that it had been built, bought, lived in, and lost before the garage was even finished. In the kitchen, copies of *Martha Stewart Living* and *Real Simple* were stacked on the counter next to a Rolodex of index-card recipes, a cookbook (*365 Ways to Cook Pasta*), and more recipe cards with instructions on one side and a picture of the end result—curried coleslaw! fish crepes! etc.—on the back. Christmas decorations had been set neatly near the sliding-glass door. A handful of popcorn lay scattered on the carpet. Outside, the big-screen television had been set carefully at the edge of the driveway, next to a fern. Such conscientious neatness was strangely defiant, a declaration of dignity against any transgression.

After locking up, we waved to an elderly neighbor in a bikini, who was sunning in front of her screened-in garage patio. We'd see her again in the same position the next week, when we returned for two more trash-outs on the same block—same square footage, same layout, same view, same fate.

———

THREE in the truck again, this time we tackled a battered, yellow bungalow on Suwanee Avenue, on a block crowded with big, arthritic oaks shading early-century cottages. We were, according to the map, in an anonymous zone, a toss-up between the south end of Seminole Heights and the north end of Tampa Heights, a pair of subdivisions that sprouted at the opening of the twentieth century, and which, in a century's time, evolved into landmarked historic enclaves tucked within Tampa's sprawl, with plaques nailed to the porches. The houses here on Suwanee were just as architecturally relevant as those throughout the landmarked blocks, and certainly as old, but were shabby. The block reflected more grit than charm or history, with no zoning to shield it from the loading bays of a defunct supermarket and a fireworks factory across the street. There must have been a rustic elegance to this neighborhood when these houses were built, between the tenures of Taft and Coolidge, when the avenue itself lacked a name and was still just dirt. All that was left now was a funky, bygone beauty.

Hector trudged up to the front porch—plastic camera in his pocket, hammer in one hand and flathead in the other. Ismael followed him. I lagged behind, eating bread and coffee as I walked, just to get something in my stomach. Hector reached the front door, crouched, and began to work on the lock, and in a few minutes was able to shove through. Just a few steps behind him, still eating, mouth full, I waded into a cocktail stench of bread and butter and piss and mold. I turned and marched back out onto the porch for air, and to finish and swallow, but the odor was wafting out ahead of me by now. I threw the bread into the bushes and walked back to the truck.

The street was peaceful, and I sipped and listened: to the moan of a mourning dove, to Hector huffing at Ismael inside the house. In between his curses, the plastic camera cranked and clicked, amplified, slightly, by the hollow rooms. Half the pictures would be compromised by a broken finger he couldn't quite control, which he could never quite coax out of the frame, so that, lit by the flash, it intruded like a bright blob in the corner of every shot. My father cursed this specter every time he saw it.

Ismael returned to fetch a mallet. When he reached the truck he stood on his toes to try to peek inside the tool chest, but struggled. "Help me," he said. "You're taller."

I told him to relax a minute, let Hector work in peace, let the house air out. Ismael sighed, looked back, then went to the front seat and grabbed his thermos, and poured himself a capful of coffee. Birds sang in long chirps, a stretched note, like the worn-out brakes of a heavy beater. To the east, the interstate frothed low and calm with distant traffic. The peacefulness was a primer for small talk, which never stood a chance between us in Hector's presence. I watched Ismael sip his coffee and stare up at the canopy of leaves, at the street, at nothing in particular. In all the years we'd worked together, off and on, I'd never asked him how he ended up with this gig. I still knew very little about him, and what I knew was pieced sloppily together from my father's half-remembered tales. And so I asked him.

He came to America twice, he said, first in 1952, landing in the farming town of Immokalee, Lee County, where his brother lived, just east of the Corkscrew Swamp. "I did a bit of every-thing," he said. "I was here in Florida picking tomato, picked cot-ton in Georgia, went to Michigan to pick cherry. Work in Ohio. Went to South Carolina to pick tomato. Wash dishes in Nueva York. Live in Philadelphia. The second time, things were good in Puerto Rico. I had a house there. A wife. But I started fucking around with other women, and my wife found out. She told me it was time to go. So I packed a bag and left. I came and stayed with my brother."

"Would you ever go back? Retire, maybe?"

"I'll never go back," he said.

Hector shouted for his mallet.

"This guy has no patience," Ismael said.

"Dad says you used to get into some fights back in Puerto Rico," I said.

"Yeah," he said, nonchalant. "I went to jail about . . . eight times."

The mallet was missing, or we simply couldn't find it, so Ismael walked over to the trailer, grabbed a sledgehammer, and sauntered back into the house.

It turned out that neither the mallet nor the sledgehammer would suffice. The oaks around back had begun to fall apart, and one limb, thick as a lightpost, had dropped and crushed the eave above the kitchen door, pressing the door shut. We decided to tackle the backyard first, dispose of the limb and clean the rest of the yard while the house breathed.

Hector pulled the truck and trailer around back, drawing up just past the alley, then jackknifing the truck in reverse, trailer first, down the alley and, after a deft, sharp left, into the yard. The trailer snapped whatever stood in its way. Hector was acrobatic in reverse, never pausing, and without so much as a scratch on the truck. He could've backed the thing into a doghouse if he needed to.

I fetched the chainsaw for him, brought it over to where he stood by the limb, and stood back as he yanked the thing alive. With the chainsaw shivering in one hand, he reached with the other for a twig that blocked his angle, snapped it, then bent over and squeezed the chainsaw's trigger, slicing at the smaller branches with a brutal quickness, almost hacking at them, clearing a space to work on the fatter limb that had crushed the door. He went at it, shards of wood spitting out of the cleft dug out by the loud blade. He practically shoved that huffing saw through the branch until it buckled and thudded against the dirt.

I cradled the diced-up pieces, thick as pony kegs, and began hauling them over to the trailer, one after another onto a pile of twigs and rubbish that added a crackle to the *bonk* of each concussion. The chainsaw buzzed and gurgled; the dog across the alley went berserk.

We tamed what we could in an hour—lugging the tree in pieces, raking up the leaves, scraping the compost off the brick. Rousing the worms, squashing beetles. The yard grew brightly mottled as the sun climbed higher.

In that moment, in the knotted shade of the yard, I loved this work. Here the humid mess, the decay, the dew and gunk, reigned peacefully, revealing small, wondrous intersections of man and nature: Where the chain-link fence had been set too close to an oak, the trunk had swallowed it, the bark folding like calcified lava around the metal post; where a dark puddle had formed in the crease of a crumpled, blue kiddie pool, frogs had gathered. Our thick plastic garbage bags crackled as we peeled them open, and magnified the rustle of the leaves as we smashed them down. Lizards scuttled along the wheels of the truck. The yard was a respite from the Levittown wastelands we'd been cleaning out all week. The landscape wasn't manicured; nature was holding firm—was slowly winning, judging by the canopy of limbs crossing high above us. We were in the city, in a ghetto outright, with traffic well within earshot, but the oaks and moss and dregs had formed a place of their own. This job was hardly ever romantic, but here, at least, it felt as if we'd suspended the rush, and paused in a sublime little corner of the city's gone natural world.

Nature had been assigned its proper domestic place long before this house was built (the Craftsman bungalow is, after all, just a simple shelter made handsome with its touch of flair). But those old bungalows and their porches were telling. They artic- ulated nature's complicated assignment to be impressive but not invasive, to cooperate with the home from a comfortable dis- tance. These porches were the transitional space between the comfort inside and the forces without, stages for atmosphere—a cool morning, a lovely dusk, a view of the lake, a front seat to a storm—that evolved by the demands of cost and fashion into sunrooms, screened-in pools, and sliding-glass doors (thousands of which have been rendered useless by that telltale Florida remodeling phenomenon, the patio enclosure, or the Florida Room). Something even as simple as a window, from those in air-conditioned Florida Rooms to the sealed picture windows of climate-controlled condominiums, speaks to this flirtation with nature, extracting what suits a dweller while keeping the rest in check.

This assignment, critical to living comfortably, makes the foreclosure a marvelous natural phenomenon. In a foreclosure, nature breaks through like a quiet, patient predator. With enough time, interiors morph into a semblance of the outside world, into household landscapes that provide the same aesthetic shock as the weirdly magnetic images of post-Katrina New Orleans or post-meltdown Chernobyl: portraits of nature's usurpation of the man-made stuff, a revolt against the will to tame it. Ultimately, the magnetism of the foreclosure has as much to do with the irrelevance of a missing owner as it does with that owner's piecemeal history strewn about. Inside, amid the rot, the brevity of human life is juxtaposed against geological time, against the pace and breadth of what surrounds us. A sound and fury interrupted. In that rot, in the inevitable, inexorable encroachment of the forces a house was designed to keep out, lies the slow, mute power of death, of time, of God. So we swat at flies while gazing through a window at the weather; but leave a house alone long enough, and flies will find a way in. Mold will spread. An underworld will seep to the surface and thrive.

These same forces turned that small backyard into a divine communion, underscored by a bit of recent literary luck. Just before my arrival in Florida I'd spotted and borrowed from a friend's home a book of poems by Theodore Roethke, and discovered a language I'd lacked to describe the strange pleasure and revulsion of this job. I already knew "My Papa's Waltz," and could still recognize, as an adult, the giant mysteriousness of a father as Roethke renders his own in that poem. But in poems such as "Root Cellar" and "Cuttings" and "Forcing House," it was the theme that ran alongside patrimony—the rich intractability of the natural world (of life and death, rot and splendor) that seeped through the cracks as forcibly as what was unspoken between fathers and sons—that made Roethke the patron saint of this work my father and I shared. I recognized his dangling bulbs and searching roots, his "congress of stinks!" that, in my case, stifled a kitchenette. I, too, knew rooms "dank as a ditch" and air "ripe as old bait." I had dug into loamy refrigerators. I had kneeled and crawled in homes where ultimately you learned that, despite the void and the fallout, somewhere underneath the carpet and in between the Sheetrock, things were moving—slowly, but moving nonetheless; and that, despite the life evaporated by ruin, two cycles—natural and invented—never stopped revolving at their respective paces. In our work, we fed on this disaster, and ultimately repaired it into something suitable for the next host. And you could regard the unstoppable cycles any way you wanted—as apathetic or regenerative, unsympathetic or inching toward an upswing—but the cycles kept moving. These forces, economic and natural, simply did not stop.

Into the trailer went the crumpled kiddie pool, the water bottles and beer cans, all unburied from underneath the detritus. We tossed fronds and cables, lugged away rocks and pieces of trunk. As Ismael and I dragged our rakes across the backyard, stuffing years of leaves into our bags, the scraping began to sing a little: concrete. A patio lay underneath that carpet of earth.

Within a couple of hours we'd restore some order to the yard, reclaiming it for the purposes of real estate—spruced up, sure, but not quite as thrilling, not nearly as beautiful. And as we raked, Ismael sang to himself, a nostalgic anthem he sang often and to no one, cooing softly, *"Buenos días, Puerto Rico . . ."*

———

THE oaks, the moss: It's tempting to sentimentalize the world they summon, to imagine from the comfortable distance of five hundred years a natural pageantry that preceded the gaudy signage of Nebraska Avenue. But it's foolish to assume that the tragedy of Tampa's sprawl lies entirely in a lost idyllic wealth. The hammocks here and there, where early lots were platted for the shade, suggest an Eden, but whether Tampa or Florida was a paradise before the booms-and-busts began in earnest depends on whom you ask—a naturalist or entrepreneur, an ecologist or contractor.

By many accounts, before Henry Plant arrived in the 1880s—linking his railroad empire to the water, then building an extravagant hotel to lure the fin de siècle wealth of wintering elite—Tampa was, for the most part, an awful place for a settlement, a sanctuary for birds and toads. Calusa Indians found a harmony in these forests, but how they did so remains largely a mystery (neither the Spanish nor the English nor the American settlers bothered to learn their secret). Between the hapless Pánfilo de Narváez's landing in Tampa Bay in 1528 and the three hundred years that followed—as Florida was handed off from Spain to England and back to Spain again, and then, in 1821, officially territorialized by the United States—Tampa was little more than a sopping, impossible topography. Florida as a whole intimidated more people than it beckoned, and the farmers and ex-cons who sought a livelihood from its soil paid dearly for the effort. By the middle of the nineteenth century, when many Americans were pushing westward, and the rest of the country was invigorated by ideas of reinvention, Florida was largely regarded as "worthless" and "uninhabitable." Very few even considered descending to Florida—this, despite the best effort of such promotions as one from the *New York Times* in 1852, which promised such internal resources as "sugar, cotton, lumber, tobacco, tropical fruit, the olive, Sisal-hemp, and arrowroot," not to mention fisheries that were "a mine of wealth . . . rivaling those of the Grand Banks and the Bay of Fundy." Plenty of resources, yes, but the problem was triggering a large-scale interest. Compared to reports in the *Times* of "Indian butcheries" committed by Chief Billy Bowlegs and various tribes of a "blood-thirsty character," those Florida press releases just weren't all that convincing.

Settlers did make a go of it, but found an implacable enemy in the palmetto—the low, spiky frond the Spanish cursed in various accounts (which my father warned me of as a child by tapping his finger on the tip of its leaf, then holding up his finger as it bled). William Bartram, the eighteenth-century horticulturalist, encountered walls of this "sword plant" that were "as impenetrable to man, or any other animal, as if they were a regiment of grenadiers with their bayonets pointed at you," growing so thick that "a rat or bird can scarcely pass through them." Even so, Bartram admitted that the palmetto was a "very singular and beautiful production."

Bartram's *Travels* is full of exasperation at the plant life—and Bartram didn't even go south of Ocala. But he was awestruck, too, at the wild beauty he encountered here. Florida was a land of plenty: the fragrance of flowers and orange groves; spacious shade under wide-brimmed oaks; in the evening, he and his guides had an easy time picking off a meal among the "curlews, willets, snipes" crowding the skies. He found the orange groves serene. He found the oysters, which lay in heaps along the banks and shores, addicting.

But night comes on, and more than one is spent enduring "the stings of musquetoes, the roaring of crocodiles, and the continual noise and restlessness of the sea fowl, thousands of them . . . all promiscuously lodging together, and in such incredible numbers, that the trees were entirely covered." This was a carnival landscape of raw energy, every square inch of it possessing a generous but often inhospitable beauty.

For the most part, this blend of misery and enchantment was the standard fare for the Florida settler. And yet, despite how tough the going was, despite what the land demanded, Florida's settlers were likely to be second-tier types. As John McPhee writes in *Oranges*, Florida was "the only wilderness in the world that attracted middle-aged pioneers" during the years of westward expansion. "The young ones were already on their way west to California." Even then, Florida was a magnet for the ailing—"aging doctors, retired brokers, and consumptives" for whom the temperate winter was a more reasonable calling than the gold of California.

One of those doctors was Daniel Garrison Brinton, whose 1869 *Guide-Book of Florida and the South, for Tourists, Invalids and Emigrants* is just one of many examples of a healthy literary subgenre, the Florida guidebook—mostly narrative advertorials extolling the climate, the fishing, the food (with an appendix of hotel advertisements thrown in for good measure). For the victims of pulmonary trouble, or any one of a "catalogue of maladies" inflicted upon the victims of "winter, the foe of the aged," the treatment was simple (and, in hindsight, faith-based): Go to Florida, and rest. Here the sufferers of consumption, asthma, bronchitis, scrofula, rheumatism, dyspepsia (a "hydra-headed disease"), catarrh, neuralgia, general anxiety, or just old age could find a cure in the weather, or at least die in peace. And for those couples who had trouble conceiving, Brinton reminds them that "heat stimulates powerfully the faculty of reproduction." Prescription: Florida. "We can with every reason recommend to childless couples, without definite cause of sterility, a winter in the south," Brinton writes. "I have known most happy effects from it."

It was easy to get here: The five-day trip by steamship from New York to St. Augustine cost twenty-five dollars. The cheap tickets were a good start, but lured a clientele who received as much bad news as good. Florida was the weird backyard of the American imagination, as deadly as it was salubrious. Fever outbreaks were constant, and infamous, sometimes occurring as late as fall. News of Florida fevers reached readers as far away as New Zealand. No one knew what caused them, or how to cure them. The villagers of Jacksonville tried firing cannon, thinking the concussion would purify the air, like some deafening voodoo. For most of the nineteenth century, Florida remained stuck in the schizophrenic image of both a paradise and a hell. Even the name of one of the territory's largest counties, Mosquito County (renamed Orange County with statehood in 1845) said all you needed to know about what awaited you there. As one writer for the *New York Herald* put it in 1864, "No decent man would think of living in the state outside of two or three points on the St. Johns or the Gulf."

Enter the dredger. In 1881, a Philadelphia sawmaker named Hamilton Disston purchased four million acres (at twenty-five cents an acre) from a debt-strapped state on the verge of bankruptcy, promising to drain it. He cut a deal with the rail magnate Henry Plant and Standard Oil co-founder Henry Flagler to develop land along railroad routes reaching to Tampa and Key West. Modern Florida's messy, painful emergence began with these three men and the drainage effort they inaugurated. As steamship routes were cut along the Kissimmee River, developers began to channel billions of gallons eastward and westward from Lake Okeechobee, the enormous body of water like a gun-shot wound in Florida's belly, to help dry the lands to the south and begin taming the Everglades. Beginning in Jacksonville, Flagler scored a line of railroad along the East Coast, eventually reaching the peninsula's southernmost tip. Plant, meanwhile, slashed through the middle of the state, with a terminus at the port of Tampa, an anemic village of about seven hundred souls winnowed by twenty years of yellow fever, but a key port for connecting with steamships bound for Havana.

Plant was already a tycoon in the making when he first visited Florida, during a convalescence prescribed for his wife's tuberculosis. They spent a few months at a villa on the St. Johns River, and it was there, in a much friendlier part of the state, where Plant imagined Florida's potential. His wife would eventually succumb to her chronic illness; to abate his loss, Plant dove into his work. After the Civil War and the 1873 economic depression that followed, dozens of railroad companies went into bankruptcy, which allowed Plant to acquire several railroad lines cheap, developing all those defunct tracks into a transportation empire that shuttled parcels and passengers across the South, comprising 2,100 miles of track, a dozen steamboats, and eight hotels.

Tampa's first boom came in the summer of 1883, when hundreds of rail workers descended to finish Plant's extension of the Florida Line. An economy formed: boardinghouses and dry-goods stores, sawmills and vendors. Within just a few months the line was finished, and steamships began ferrying tourists to Havana.

But yellow fever persisted. In the fall of 1887, it killed almost eighty, and crippled about seven hundred more. The citizens set tar barrels on fire at every intersection; they, too, fired cannon. By the new year, there was an exodus, and real estate plummeted.

As a response, to save his city, Plant provided a stimulus, building a luxury hotel on the Hillsborough River—a tribute to the
Moorish palace, in fashion at the end of the nineteenth century:
more than five hundred rooms, electricity, phones, European
sculpture in the lobby, Venetian mirrors, no frill spared. Plant's
train pulled up to the west porch to unload guests. The sprawling Orthodox-revival was a shrewdly placed stopover for those
bound for Havana, more an economic decision than one based
on the natural beauty of the setting. Yes, there was a river view,
but the grounds were heavily landscaped, a manufactured tropical beauty that replaced the piney muck he encountered. The
hotel offered an economic shock to Tampa's slumber, registering
four thousand guests in its first two months. It booked between
December and April, then shuttered for the unbearably hot
months. The only exception came in 1898, during the Spanish-
American War, when the hotel was used as quarters for officers
and the press corps. Theodore Roosevelt and his coterie of officers strategized from rockers on the porch while foot soldiers
sweated it out on the grounds. Thirty thousand soldiers set up
camp on both sides of the river, performed drills, wrote home
about the weather, and spent a considerable amount of effort surviving Tampa. Bugs, fever, and a broiling heat made for a night-
marish prelude to the fighting. Boredom and food poisoning
compounded the misery. The wool uniforms in June were just an
added absurdity. The fish were big, but they offered little solace.
"Tampa is, collectively speaking, a BUM place," wrote one sol-
dier. "Some of the boys are writing home about the oranges and
the bananas and all that. But they are twice as good and twice as
cheap in Washington." It was a popular war, to be sure, but hardly
worth its price. All told, more than three hundred soldiers died

in combat, with nearly that many dying from disease while await-
ing deployment in Florida's camps.

Eventually, a city staggered out of the wild. Lots were platted in
shady groves, and then, once all the shade was taken, platted
everywhere else. Since Reconstruction, the narrative of Tampa
continued to reflect the narrative of Florida writ large: growth,
which accelerated exponentially after the Great Wars, so that
growth itself became the backbone of a sunshine economy. Beginning with the economic prosperity that followed World War II,
Florida's population doubled in twenty years, from 3 million to
6 million, then nearly doubled again over the next twenty. And
with each boom since Plant's arrival, Tampa regenerated through
an almost obsessive scraping away of itself, a constant revision,
such that, growing up here, there was little sense of feeling
anchored.

Florida is a transitory place comprising different rates of
motion: people fleeing tougher climates, or migrating from over-
seas; visitors staying for a week or a winter, for a lifetime or what's
left of it. The cliché is that Florida is where you go to rest, or
succumb to life's last slow, hot fade. But in the half century or
so since the postwar boom, Florida has added contradicting layers to its hot, lethargic reputation. In all the time I've lived here,
come and gone and visited, I've cursed how Florida, despite the
ease it advertises, possesses so little stability. Tampa in particular
is characterized by a commercial fluidity, and this matters,
because the signage, whether you like it or not, becomes a part
of the landscape in memory. But the merchants come and go,
the mom-and-pops weaken quickly. Even the big-box "anchor"
stores seem impatient. Highways and bridges are under endless

construction, an infrastructure always half-finished. The entire landscape is under revision, ten square miles of the state disappearing every day.

Thus, Florida defies its own reputation. A mecca of relaxation that never keeps still, a restlessness rooted in Hamilton Disston's mission, what became the scourge of the landscape, and eventually the ugly root word of this crisis—*development*. And with development, the promise of an easier way of life. This has always been the draw. Newspapers once claimed that orange growers on the Indian River could live "entirely upon the returns of a few large trees, spending the whole year in hunting and fishing—doing no work." Over the centuries, between the Spanish and the crowds outside the subdivision gates, were the promises all that different? The Spanish sought to step into a pile of wealth and haul it away; orange growers sought to pluck their profits standing up. By the twentieth century, the concept of the land itself bore the profit. One need not even do anything with it, just sit and wait. Or flip it. In this way, the developers whose condominiums loomed dark along the nighttime coast in 2008 were simply heirs to a tradition that included the likes of Walt Disney and the Rosen brothers and reached back to Disston and Flagler and Plant, to the days when bankruptcy gave birth to Florida as we know it, through the fire sale of swamps and railroads, to the days when those first developers, all snowbirds, began their vigorous gorging on this late-blooming state.

WE eased onto the Howard Frankland Bridge, sped up with the traffic, aiming west for the Pinellas County dump. I stared out at the choppy bay, at the green water touched with whitecaps. Ismael, next to me, read aloud from road signs to practice his English

("How is my driving?" . . . "Walmarrr."). Finally, he picked up where he'd left off on how he began working for my father.

He was a substitute, he said, a second pick after his nephew, who was an addict, succumbed to AIDS. "He was real skinny at the end," Ismael said.

"He was always skinny," Hector said. "What's important is that he accepted Christ at the end." Hector blew his nose and cleared his throat, and we knew what was next. "When a man dies, he passes into eternity. But which eternity is he going to? To hell, or to live with God? ¿*Para la Gloria*?" You crack the door with Hector and he'll kick it off the hinges. Now he soared through a diatribe that included both an excoriation of the Vatican (the pope had issued a new encyclical that week, citing excessive wealth as a deadly sin, which Hector found infuriatingly hypocritical) and a fresh if darkly Pentecostal interpretation of the story of the Ark, in which thousands of Noah's neighbors, skeptical and mocking, were left begging and banging against its hull as the waters rose around them. Noah apparently enjoyed this brutal vindication.

I stared across the bay, where the smokestacks of Florida Power & Light rose behind the mangrove thickets on the St. Pete side— toward Weedon Island, where, as teenagers, we'd disappear on Saturday nights to drink and whip bottles into the water, and stumble around in the weedy mud. We were proud of the ritual: cars and beer and a dank barrier island none of us saw in the daytime, drinking and slapping at the no-see-ums that even in September bit and vanished and left us twitching like schizophrenics. Sure, the bugs were a hassle, but on Saturdays we claimed that place as ours, with its birdcalls and shadowy junk made all the more mysterious by the moonlight, and we made the best of it.

Among the 140 agents working out of the RE/MAX office in Palm Harbor, two carried the majority of foreclosure sales that year. Mena was one of them; Joe Koebel was the other.

Koebel's office sat tucked halfway down a long, bleached-white hallway lined with county maps, across from the break station: two desks, one near the window and piled with manila folders, the other desk set against the opposite wall, where he sat hunkered over a laptop talking on his cell phone, using an ear-piece that allowed him to type and e-mail with both hands, both of which he desperately needed.

It was mid-morning, and Koebel looked bloodshot. He darted back and forth between his desks with the busy poise of a knife juggler. We talked in between phone calls—on his cell, the land line—all of which he answered, no matter that he screened each one. Now and then he'd give me a look to suggest the seriousness or foolishness of a call—an oblivious retiree looking to sell during what was obviously a glut in the market; his handyman updating him on which swimming pools were still green and which were clear, which condos were ready, et cetera. And no matter how much a question seemed to try his patience, he was always polite.

He paused, lowered his face into his hands, reacting to something—bad news on the screen or the other end of his cell phone conversation, I couldn't tell which. I looked around the room at his effects: portraits of weekend football pals, of his wife and daughters, of friends and relatives; a box of Flutie Flakes and other Buffalo memorabilia; an electronic fart-noise maker, about the size of a pager. Above him on the wall hung a portrait of the Three Stooges on the links, posing on the eighteenth green. On the wall behind me, a greaseboard covered with addresses, top to bottom, of the thirty or so foreclosures in rotation, their progress marked by green, blue, or red ink. Green meant closed, meant money, and there was precious little green on the board the day I showed up.

Koebel looked at me again to signal an apology, promising to end the call soon. The look of his eyes—puffed, weighed down, the skin underneath a little darker—was just one effect of the hours he'd spent staring at a screen, reading maps, scanning numbers. Numbers were his obsession; he'd gleaned an ethical lesson from their calculation, but seemed more bewildered than righteous about what he found. The incessant question of the spring was: Who was to blame? That question was the natural by-product of a disaster of this proportion, but the size of the damage also meant that its causes were various. Culpability netted a dizzying number of the guilty—mortgage brokers, seller's agents, people who knew what they were doing and those who didn't, those who took a chance and those who were duped.

Of course, the most egregious numbers told the clearest stories. "Look at tax rolls on a property," he said, without missing a beat after hanging up the call. "You'll see where people took a loan out for $300,000 in 2006 and then went into foreclosure. What's that telling me? It's telling me they pulled the equity out knowing that the market was bad. How could they take out a $300,000 loan, and then that property's foreclosed on a year later? Do the math. If you borrowed $300,000, with taxes and insurance your payment's going to be at least $3,500 a month. You would *know* that. In my opinion, they knew the market was depressed. They knew they couldn't sell the house, so they went ahead and refinanced it, and then tried to do a short sell. Over the years of looking at paperwork, I can see it."

His handyman was calling, and he interrupted himself to take the call. "Is it clear, pumps working and everything?" he said, staring at me. "Right. You gave me the bill on that and I've got it in front of me. What color's the water? Really? I gotta get a picture next day or two when it's clear to show that it's all done. Okay. See ya."

He rolled his chair to the left and picked up another folder. "Look here," he said, bending the folder open. "These people bought on the come, I'm taking a guess—a condo in Clearwater Beach. The condo market was such a craze here for the past five years that if you bought in 2001, put $20,000 down, and the condo was built in late 2002 or early 2003, you made a hundred grand before you even closed. People were selling their escrow—'double closing.' They were closing their loan in the morning, selling to a new buyer for $100,000 more by the afternoon. The fuckin' *mayor* did it."

He grabbed a folder. "These people," he said, running his finger down the sum column of a single page on a thick stack, "they paid $728,000 for this condo in 2006. Look at the loan history. Here's a loan for $70,000 from American Brokers; here's a loan for

$582,000, which makes $650,000 of loan. Now, they must have refinanced here for $671,000 through Lehman Brothers. They took out *another* fuckin' loan for $224,000! So they owed $895,000 on $728,000!" He rolled his chair back, put his hands up. "I can't speak for these people," he said, "but do the math. Looks like they probably put in maybe a hundred grand, they took the equity out, they got their hundred grand back, and they probably walked because they couldn't sell it. That's a total guess on my part. But look at the numbers. It's a foreclosure, a ding on their credit. But they don't give a shit because they're from New York State"— meaning that the home in question was a second property, and likely expendable. "They're untouchable," he said.

His phone vibrated, the handyman again. A condominium was ready for inspection. Koebel invited me to come along to see it. We climbed into his SUV, tagged with a Buffalo Bills vanity plate, the backseat strewn with crumpled maps, and drove through fast traffic for forty minutes to a Tuscan-themed apartment complex, a condo conversion during the boom. The unit we were after was on Chianti Place. The place was empty, clean. The smoke alarm chirped, its battery fading. Koebel shuttled from room to room, taking pictures. I asked him if he'd ever run into awkward situations, confrontations, anything of that sort.

"Strangest thing I came across," he said, "I got to this one house, every piece of furniture was intact. The closets were filled, the baby's room had everything in it. The bed was in the master bedroom. Even the table was set. I open up the stove, gnats come flying out." He called the sheriff's office and asked a detective to track down the previous owners, to see if they still wanted any of what they'd left behind. "They were somewhere in Canada," he said. "A lady calls me back, and I asked her what she wanted me to do with all the stuff. She said, 'Let me ask my husband, I'll call you back.'" And that was it. "Gave it all away," Koebel said. "Dining room set, gold jewelry, all of it."

He took his pictures, and offered to swing by and pick up lunch for us on the way back to the office—nothing fancy, just time for a drive-through. He forecasted the experience for me: "Go to the drive-through, get it, shove it down in about one-point-five seconds on the way back to the office." Was today especially busy? "Well, usually my wife helps out at the office, but she's not around today, so things are *slightly* more hectic. But that's how it is. That's how I am. I'm the gerbil inside the cage, spinning the wheel. I'm a grunt, I'm a worker, I'm a mole, I'm a worker ant, worker bee, whatever you want to call it."

We pulled up to a Wendy's, pausing at the end of the drive-through line of cars. Just the act of stopping there, a couple cars shy of the menu board, was a respite. He sighed.

"Have you ever burned out?"

"So far, a handful of times."

The cell phone rang. "Yeah, hon, go ahead. Just get the light hairball control. If they have the big bag of Kitty Litter, get that. Okay, love you. 'Bye. Hello, this is Joe. Yeah, it's ready. On Durney. The code is OCN. October Charlie Nancy. Did you send them all off? Did you already send off the one on IAS? Okay."

Back in his office, each of us at a desk, devouring cheeseburgers with the foil spread flat, we talked a bit about his start in real estate. Koebel left Buffalo for Los Angeles in 1981, worked at a dry cleaners for several years, then got into air-conditioning systems for the next couple or so. He got his broker's license in 1987. "I wasn't very good at it," he mumbled, "so I started doing foreclosure BPOs, a job *nobody* wanted to do—you know, drive by, take a picture of a house, fill out a form for about an hour and a half, get a check six weeks later for fifty bucks." He filed about ten BPOs a week, and eventually began selling the foreclosures he was documenting, though not enough to make a living. To compensate for his lack of income, he lived on credit cards, amassing massive debt. Then, in a cruel twist, a car accident led to legal bills and restitution, and eventually, in 1992, as his debt overwhelmed him, bankruptcy. "I was a stupid kid," he said. "I was having a hard time, could borrow money at eighteen percent. Who knew I was never going to pay it back? Why was I so stupid? Caught up in California keeping up with the Joneses." It was enough to put a lot of things in perspective, he said. It seemed to give him a sense of ironic humility. "I'm fortunate there are foreclosures," he admitted, "because I'm making a living now. That wasn't always the case."

His assistant called. A foreclosure on Loquat Avenue would be going to the upcoming auction—a big blowout of foreclosures to be staged at the convention center—and was available for viewing that Saturday, when potential buyers would be scouring the Bay Area with catalogs in hand, looking for a bargain. She needed the lockbox code and address, which Joe spat back without pause, his mind a database of numbers and combinations. He had just a handful of houses registered with the auction. Most of them had already received short-sale offers from interested buyers—offers that reflected a home's current market value rather than what had been borrowed against its value a year ago, and well below what the bank was owed. But these were offers in an otherwise frozen market that would have spared a bank tens of thousands of dollars required to file a foreclosure with the court. And the maddening mystery that spring, among agents and homeowners both, was why the banks insisted on turning these offers down.

"This is the greed I'm talking about," Koebel said, "and the auction is a big part of it. I had two houses. One was purchased for $400,000. One was purchased for $395,000. I had offers on both of them prior to them going to auction, one for $220,000, one for $218,000. The bank turned them both down. At the auction, one sold for $175,000; the other sold for $180,000. They lost about $40,000 collectively on those houses, when I had real human being buyers—not investors—wanting to buy these homes to live in them. They ended up selling them to investors for $40,000 *less* at the auction. Because the money is tied into a portfolio or a package, so they just dump it."

He went back to his stack of sheets, scanning. Somewhere behind those numbers were tucked myriad clues to the maneuvers people made to buy, sell, trade upward, or dump a property. Of course, the numbers, no matter how closely they were pored over, couldn't tell the entire story. The numbers could never fully divulge the human element in all those transactions—the motives, the ignorance or the malice, or even the bad luck that followed. But it was a sure bet that a good portion of the fallout grew out of whatever was unspoken on the day most papers were signed, whatever had been left out of the mortgage broker's monologue, left hidden in the fine print.

Now Koebel saw it all as a reckoning that was overdue. "When a mortgage guy comes to you and says, 'Look, your ratios are a little big, but don't worry about it. I'll get you the loan,' the guy might fib and say your payments are going to be $1,200, and you think, 'Oh, I can afford that.' But he doesn't tell you that after you add the taxes and insurance, it's $1,700. And then you're sitting there at closing, and what are you going to do? You're not going to be a *man* and not close? Or are you gonna close?"

W eeks had passed without response from the owner on Hillsborough Lane, the owner of that mythic rottweiler, and the cash-for-keys offer was now off the table. The time had come for eviction. Arrangements were made. The sheriff's deputy posted a notice. A couple of days later, we arrived to follow through.

Deputies tended to be steeled (and armed) for this ritual. We were not, nor were we eager to act as muscle for the bank, or be seen as such. But by default and association and simple logic, this was the role we played on eviction day if the owner happened to be home.

I had worked only one eviction prior to this one, during my first stint, in '98. I was changing the front-door lock when the owner snuck up behind me, after I thought he had left, shuffling along the concrete walk and with his hand outstretched. I wasn't sure exactly what was in it, and maybe he saw I was startled, because he paused, and shook a set of keys, and apologized about surprising me like that—but would I be interested in buying his car? A rusted-out Oldsmobile sitting on blocks in the driveway. Six hundred. I said thank you, *thank you*, but no, I really didn't need it, and disappointment merely flitted across his face before he turned and walked off, as if he could afford no more than a moment of frustration or sadness before having to begin calculating his next move, and meanwhile humble about it all, a kindness that humiliated and infuriated me for being the one who held the lock that shut him out of his own house, a job I finished in a nervous sweat.

My father has witnessed much worse. At one eviction, the deputy knocked. A middle-aged man answered. My father remembers that he seemed unsurprised at the news, but that he asked for a minute or two to collect his things. He ducked back inside, leaving the door open, and walked back to the bedroom, where he sat on the edge of the bed, put a pistol in his mouth, and pulled the trigger.

This time, it was a cold-snap morning. Hector was home with a bad toe, and the job was left to the three of us—Ismael, my father, and me. We arrived early and parked up the street. A jackhammer rattled a few blocks away; traffic on Nebraska was a whisper. We walked through the gate and across the yard, over the chain that snaked and hooked to the buried dumbbell, past the empty plywood doghouse, and up to the door.

My father whispered, "What do you think?"

Ismael, somewhat oblivious, opened the screen door as if to get started.

"No, no, no, no," my father said. Ismael read a sign on the door: "Be-ware off de doch."

"*Esperemos por el sheriff,*" my father told him, and we moved away from the door.

"Why don't we just knock?" I said, irritated by both the weather and the suspense.

"Because *he* will," my father said of the sheriff. "We don't want to get shot. He has a gun. We don't."

"*Mi madre, qué frío,*" Ismael said.

I felt a pinch on my ankle and slapped at it, and saw Ismael slapping at his own leg, and noticed my father, too, reaching for his shin, and all of a sudden we realized that fleas, starving, were beginning to feast on us. Within seconds it felt like we were walking through a skillet of popping grease.

The deputy arrived to find us all with our pants rolled up, bending groggily up and down like a scratching calisthenics. He laughed. "I walked in there to stick the notice up the other day and they just crawled all over me," he said, passing by us into the yard. He was tall and pale and didn't look especially athletic or even all that tough. He was rather pear-shaped, really, but he was cold tempered, and didn't seem like the kind of fellow who repeated himself too often.

His knock was loud and simple, with a short salutation: "Sheriff's office. Eviction." We waited ten seconds. "All right," he said, "do your thing."

My father kneeled at the door and shoved the flathead on the shaft, slipped the scraper in, pried, and it was that easy, door open.

"Very good," the deputy said, slightly impressed, and slipped into a darkness backlit by a kitchen window, veiled in gossamer, and splotched with shadows as the sun crawled through branches, then through the curtains, to just barely touch the dull linoleum. A damp, warm funk wafted out as he moved through the doorway. We followed him inside, adjusting to the lack of light, creeping past an enormous television that blocked the front window. All we could make out at first were shadowy mounds and piles, and then I could see the short distance to the kitchen and noticed white plastic jumbo cups scattered across the counter, dishes piled up, cabinets flung open, and suddenly saw why, despite the open front door, the light failed in here: The walls, once white, were leopard-spotted in black and green. My father passed me with his camera and began clicking, and the brief pulse of the flash snapped the rooms into view. The deeper we waded toward the back, the more rancid the air became. There were boxes everywhere, half-packed—in the bedrooms, amid standing fans and clothes and papers on the floor; amid unshaded lamps; flanked by giant stuffed tigers and framed photos of babies and other loved ones; amid lightbulbs, stuffed sheep, Bibles, mothballs, red high heels, portraits of panthers, and a typewriter stuffed with neckties. It was as if, in that preparation for escape, thoughts had piled up and suffocated the mind.

The fleas were incredible. We were being devoured by them. We didn't know it then, but it would take four attacks with several gallons of poison to destroy them, an exhausting discovery each time we returned ready to work, and each time realizing, not ten steps onto the property, that another wave of blood-suckers had hatched. For now, we were simply relieved to have avoided a confrontation.

After a stop at Home Depot, and then at the Krispy Kreme nearby, Ismael and I returned to attack the fleas. I handed Ismael a sprayer, with orders to soak the yard, which he began doing, and I dragged my socks up over my jeans and went back inside to set the fumigators.

George, eighty-seven, lived next door, and came out to observe what we were up to. Under the small shade of his New York

Giants cap, from behind thick glasses, he filled me in on the man who had lived here. "He a deacon," George said. "Been in prison but cleaned up. He come over and we talk Christ talk." He wasn't sure when he'd see him next. He was surprised to see that his neighbor had lost the house. "I knew he borrowed a little bit of money, but we didn't talk too much about that."

I left my number with him on a scrap of paper, and in our small talk learned that George had been raised nearby, when this end of Tampa was still mostly rural. He left at sixteen, he said, a departure prompted by a white boy half-blinding him with an avocado pit ("This eye is cooked," he said, pointing to the left one.). There was nothing the law would do for him, so he fled to New York, where, already good at the saxophone, he started gigging with the musicians on the bop scene and shortly wound up in James Brown's first band. Was he sure about that? He promised it was true. When the band hit the Chitlin' Circuit, George, terrified of the South, quit. He moved upstate instead, janitored, got a music-teaching gig, retired, and came home again. He bought a condo from a friendly Jewish guy, he said, who gave him good advice; he sold it when the time was right, and used the profit to buy this house, nothing extraordinary, and not all that different from the deacon's except that it was freshly painted, with a tight roof, a trim yard with a flower bed, and paid for in full. He didn't owe anyone a penny, he said, and because of this freedom he was the envy of his debt-saddled children.

A haggard-looking woman approached us from across the street, her hair brown and long and ratted. "You got any metal or anything you wanna get rid of? Like stoves, 'frigerator, whatever doesn't work?"

"Sure," I told her, "but we're going to bomb it first. We'll be back tomorrow to take the stuff out."

"This gentleman," she said, and pointed to the house behind her, "his name is Pops. He'll take old fencing or whatever."

"Hey!" Pops yelled from his driveway. "Y'all rentin' that house?"

The lady shouted at him. "He said that if he's got anything like *metal* or *'frigerators* or *whatever*, he'll let you know tomorrow." Pops was a junkman, apparently, who made his living recycling metal, and it was all but a blessing to let him haul the metal away: less for us to carry, less to pay for at the dump. Fine, I said, and told him not to worry. We would toss every piece of metal we found right here in the yard, where the dumbbell was, and he could have at it. But first we needed to kill the fleas.

Pops's lady friend observed the flea situation. "Sevin dust," she said. "It chokes 'em. It kills 'em out. And if you got fresh oranges and you throw that dust and you cut some oranges up and throw it—"

"The peel is what kill 'em," Pops said. "My grandmama used to put a buncha orange peel—*hey! George!* Where you been, man?"

Pops had been standing next to George this whole time and only just now noticed him. They lived just twenty yards from each other, but you'd have thought it was a homecoming.

I looked over at Ismael, who was busy soaking the ground with that poison, and every time he felt a pinch, he'd spray himself—his legs, his hands, even his torso—and in the breeze I could see the mist of poison, lit by sunlight, waft toward his head.

"Keep it down!" I told him, but by the time he was done, he was dizzy, and in pain, and mumbling that he needed a nap.

"Pops wants first dibs on that metal," the lady friend said.

"A lot of junkmen come around," Pops said.

I nodded. "He'll get it."

———

George must have followed through on his promise to share my number. About a week later, the deacon called. His name was Joe Logan. I explained who I was, that I was writing about foreclosures, that I'd been in his house with a crew to clean it out, that I wanted to meet. He suggested a Denny's not too far from the house.

The next morning, at the Denny's on Fowler Avenue, I sat and waited, ordered coffee, then saw him: a black man near middle age, not big but solid, and clean-headed, his thick glasses fighting back the daylight coming in from outside. It wasn't until he sat down opposite me that I noticed the stillness in his eyes, as if some heaviness had settled his stare. His voice was grizzled and gentle. He didn't want food, only coffee. A baby squawked in the booth across the room.

I couldn't bring myself to ask him about what I'd found—the spots, the piles, the chaos in there. I asked very few questions, in fact, and instead let him walk me through what had happened, interrupted now and then by the waitress . . .

"When I bought my home, I had just got out of prison, after doing eighteen years. I was sentenced for drugs in the federal system. Distribution, cocaine. I was raised up in a good home. It had nothing to do with parents. Men are just gonna be men. I chose that life and I had to pay that price.

"But when I got out, things changed. I got saved, and after about two years I was set aside to be a deacon. My pastor brought me before the church, and they approved me. People notice you, your faithfulness, the way you've changed. Even my parole officer did. He went to my pastor and said they was going to put me up for early termination. So they took me off parole.

"I got a job. I was a fabricator—glass mechanics. We made sliding-glass doors, windows. And, you know, I always wanted my own home. It meant that I was trying to do the right thing, not only in society but to myself. I never owned a home, and to have worked and accomplished this *by yourself—to buy a home*: That means a lot. And the day you get a key to your own house, you feel like you have accomplished something, you know what I'm saying?

"So I worked, and I worked, and I looked around, and I kinda . . . some kinda way they gave me a . . . a voucher . . . to buy a house. Something in the mail. It was like somebody was saying that I could get a house worth fifty thousand dollars. Pre-approval, that's what it was. It was legit. So I went out lookin' for a house. They gave me an agent and he showed me the houses within that range, but the houses he showed me was all beat up. So I continued lookin', and I was just driving by and I seen it. It had a sale sign. So I went to the guy. They said after a year it would go from $650 to five-something a month because I was a first-time buyer. But it didn't. It went up.

"When I tried to refinance it, I told the guy that I wanted a thirty-year fixed. We did all the paperwork, talked on the phone. And when the lady came out there to do the signing, I'm looking at it and it said two-year adjustable something. I said, 'I didn't ask for this. The man told me it was going to be a thirty-year. I don't need a two-year.' She said, 'Well, you call him.' I called him, and asked him why he sent a two-year when I asked for a thirty. He said, 'No, you told me this and told me that.' I said, 'No, I got witnesses.' 'Cause when I was doing it, my boss man told me a two-year will hurt you unless you're gonna sell.

"So the *lady*. By the lady understanding me—she knew I was a God man—she said, 'Son, I'm gonna tell you this here and this off the record: Don't buy it. Don't sign those papers.' She said, 'I get paid for this, but I'm telling you 'cause you seem like a person who's bein' beat 'cause you don't know. Don't sign.'

"But within about a year I was going through a lot of turmoil. Job went under. I had a car and a truck. They came to me with a refinance deal, saying you could combine all that and make one price. You know, it sounded good, but it wasn't good."

Did he regret buying the house?

"The reason I regret buying the house is 'cause I lost on that. I could've came out better renting. But I always believe that if you can rent, you can own."

If he had another chance, given what he'd been through, would he buy another house?

"Yes, I'm working on that now. *Yes*, I want a house. Yes, I *want* a *house*. But this time, by the help of the Lord—I ain't gonna put it all on them. It's a lot of things I wouldn't do this time. If I knew, I would of never refinanced. That's what really put me in the hole. They sounded like combining all my bills was the best thing, and what I found out now is that it wasn't, 'cause in two years I would've paid off my cars, anyway. Very few people are gonna tell you something to help you in this business." He told me about an abandoned home he'd seen downtown, how he'd passed by it one day and had been wondering, since it looked unoccupied, how to go about making an offer.

"The thing I'm trying to find out, though, is how bad the foreclosures affect *my* economy. I got to read up on all that. I know it messed my credit up. But I got to find a way to try and establish it back. Matter of fact, they just put the lock on the house, what, a week ago? So now I wanna find out: Is there anything else they can do to me, as an individual? I know the house is gone, but say, for instance, in the next six months something blessed happens to me, I get some money. Can they come and get it?"

They could, though I didn't say it.

"Why didn't you respond to the cash-for-keys?"

"They never sent me none of that. No, they never told me. I don't even know how they got into the house. The house been abandoned for three months. I used to just go pick up my mail. I went back there when they told me I had to be gone by Monday. The day I wanted to move, it was raining so bad. It was Saturday, and then Sunday was raining. So you know that Monday morning, I just got some stuff from out the shed, and said, 'Whatever they do with the rest of this stuff, I ain't got time.' I got no money to put it nowhere. So I don't know what they gonna do with all that. Keep in the house, sell it, or what. Keep it furnished. I don't know. I guess the people who clean the house keep it, I don't know."

He didn't seem to understand that I had helped them put that lock on his door. And I had trouble telling him that most of what he owned was gone now, and that he should set aside any plans to buy another home, because with his income, and a foreclosure on his record, he will not own another house for a long time, if ever.

He stretched: It was time to get going. As we walked out into the parking lot, the heat stifling by now, I tried to explain again who I was and my purpose, and that I was at his home with the crew. "If there's stuff left over, they'll let you come get it if you want to get it," I said. "I could try and find out if there's stuff left over, if you want."

"Nah. I'm trying to move on. I'm fitting to start a job. A car wash."

"Where are you staying?"

"Wherever I wanna."

I told him that I'd grabbed what I could from the house to help track him down, and, walking up to my car, I reached in the back-seat for the Bible I'd found with phone numbers scribbled in the back—parole officers, friends, pastors. "And, anyway, I grabbed this and I brought it in case you wanted it."

He laughed.

"I guess that's your Bible?"

"Yes," he said, and the laugh was laced with—*pity*. "That's part of my ex-wife's stuff. Yeah, this is nice."

"If I find out if there's anything left in the house—"

"No. I don't want nuthin'. I'm through with it."

"But you left so much. Pictures and letters and—"

"It's trash."

I promised to be in touch, and that sounded fine to him. We shook hands once more and parted, and for a while I watched him in the rearview mirror as he walked away, slipping through a row of bushes onto the empty parking lot of the bank next door.

Saturday morning, cool and humid. A hundred and fifty properties were set to go on the auction block at the convention center in downtown Tampa, the first stop of the Real Estate Disposition Corporation's eight-city tour, during which the listings for about a thousand homes and condos would be rattled off like livestock to mostly tepid crowds. For the past month people had been combing the city with REDC's catalog in hand, nosing through it, following the signs. Some houses were tended to by an agent, some by a neighbor's boy, whoever had the time to sit there for eight hours while investors and the merely curious walked through, grabbed the paperwork, and checked their lists. Most of these were low-priority properties that weary agents couldn't move themselves, or didn't want to. Some were bargains, if the market held steady and the bidder didn't get trigger-happy; others seemed like moneypits; the rest were eyesores.

The main hall of the convention center was packed. Joe Koebel was there, along with a few of his clients. He looked distracted. "My guy forgot his cashier's check," he said. "I had to call a buddy of mine and do a bait-and-switch." The buddy was a man named Jeff, linebacker tall but with a voice that sounded like some parody of a grandmother from New Jersey. Jeff knew a lot about property, enough that it had become profitable for him, and I couldn't help but admire his type—an industrious fellow who had mastered the complexities of the business, and who could tear a wall down, and who had a bored swagger about it all. Even this mind-boggling crisis seemed just barely entertaining to him.

Jeff flipped through the book. "Is this your house, Joe, on Thirteenth Avenue?"

"No."

"Oh, this one was. This was the one that little kid who couldn't speak English was at."

"Yeah, Alex. The Russian kid. I paid him to sit my houses for me."

"His handwriting was phenomenal."

It was a democratic scene, almost beautifully egalitarian: twenty- and thirty-something hipsters; middle-aged fathers with earpiece phones; Chinese couples, Indian families, African Americans, elderly transplants, Hispanics; and, the closest thing to celebrity here, the cowboy investors, men who wore their wealth in gleaming, pointed boots and glimmering shirts, untucked, each one of them with a pair of sunglasses hovering at the brow, as if it were a trend of moguls. They carried themselves with a very deliberate air of relaxation.

Inside the ballroom, the auctioneer's podium was flanked by two giant screens on which rotated the planet Earth, branded with the letters REDC. The sun hovered in the galactic distance. The Commodores' "Brick House" thumped from the PA system. Chris Chamberlain, the executive vice president of REDC, trotted up to the podium to give the crowd a pep talk. "You have the perfect storm right now," he said. "Remember, folks, this is the perfect buying opportunity. If you look at real estate cycles in the last hundred years in the United States of America, every time we go into a low—which we are in the low portion of that real estate cycle right now—that represents a great buying opportunity for you. And remember, that low is not as low as the previous cycle's low. However, over a hundred years, every time the market comes storming back, the next peak has always—I repeat, *always*—exceeded the peak of the last real estate cycle. That's how money's made in real estate, folks. Buy in the low part of the cycle."

Was this an opportunity? Or just a primer for the next disaster? Chamberlain's history lesson worked as revival-tent homily, but it ignored what was changing in America's economic condition. It assumed this low part of the cycle was like any other, and it wasn't. Bear Stearns had collapsed, for one thing, which—aside from the carnage to come—suggested an economic phase much more precarious than a *lull*; it was easy to sense the threat to other institutions that would eventually unravel, a meltdown brewing for September. The "low part of the cycle" grossly understated how widespread the damage was, and how quickly it was spreading. That planet on the big screen seemed appropriate enough: Just a month earlier, six thousand angry, jeering shareholders had filled a soccer arena in Switzerland after UBS, the Swiss financial juggernaut, wrote down $37 billion in losses from securities propped up by the same sort of real estate that was on auction today. By October, mortgages like those behind the bargains on the screen would bring Iceland to its knees.

A spotter for the bids, young and tall and in a rented tux, his head shaved close, bounced on his toes, slapping the rolled-up REDC catalog against his palm. He had an athletic, almost

Pentecostal, anxiousness about him, as if waiting for something to burst, or a whistle to blow. When he or the other spotter made eye contact with the audience, they'd nod and make over-friendly, boisterous small talk. I suppose this was their way of getting the crowd loosened up.

"This is my house here," Koebel said, pointing to the catalog. He looked at the opening bid. "It isn't worth fifty thousand the way it sits, that's bullshit."

The auction began. Property No. 1, a condominium in Palm Harbor, worth $150,000 six months ago, opened at $1,000, and the emcee rattled through tens of thousands of dollars with shivering speed, reaching $60,000 in less than half a minute. When he reached $70,000 he chopped the bidding down to increments of $5,000, but didn't slow his patter down so much as repeat the bid until a card went up and a spotter yelped and pointed, then jogged across the room. When the emcee hit $80,000, the crowd kept still. The spotters grew restless, waved their hands and flicked their fingers, goading, but no one raised a card. The condo went for $75,000 in just under a minute and forty-three seconds, to the gentleman there in the middle seat. The crowd applauded. As the spotter led the winner to the stage, it was obvious the man was in a daze, shy, not quite confident in his purchase, and certainly not all that comfortable being paraded in front of hundreds of others who might have thought it was a dumb one. Eventually, the man would be led down the hall to financing, and if he qualified, the house would be taken off the list. If he didn't, they'd auction it off again.

For an hour or so the spotters gestured and shouted with a samurai flourish. It was a show, for sure, the gravitas of buying a home perverted into circus. I saw couples making out, children splayed across chairs, bored and restless. Their parents rushed back and forth with cups of coffee from the small coffee station. The spotters struck disco poses and screamed with every card that went up. The bald spotter waited by one woman for several minutes, as if she had promised him a bid but was holding back. He bounced, and goaded her, and when she nodded he let himself off his chain with a screech—*sold*, for $385,000! And when a hot property was finally bought, dozens of people headed for the door. It went on like this for hours, through 140 more properties. Out in the main hall again, we'd gathered to compare notes. Koebel was shaking his head at some of the bids he'd witnessed, at how auction fever had defeated the bargain the auction had promised in the first place.

"This is the one I thought was a joke," Jeff said, pointing. "Tangerine Street. Fifty-five thousand, it went for! I mean, it's a beautiful, brand-new home, but you can't get to or from the house without risking your life. This is, like, the number-one drug-dealing section in Clearwater! I went to look at it this morning, couldn't get out of the car. Fifty-five thousand and I couldn't get out of the car! If you rent it out as Section 8 housing, it might be a good deal. But you can't go there. They literally tackled my car trying to sell me drugs."

"The one on Belcher," a stranger piped in. "*Somebody* over-paid for that."

"That one I liked," Jeff said. "It was very clean. New windows, new tile floor. Built-in pool."

"Yeah, but that kitchen! And there was all that mold behind that wall."

"No, it was a cute little home. All you got to do is a little work on it. What'd it go for?"

"$135,000."

Jeff tilted his head and cocked a brow.

A sultry morning, well too hot for such an early hour. My father and I swung by the deacon's house to photograph it, to document its progress for the bank. Just a block away, on North Elmer Street, Hector and Ismael were handling another foreclosure. The snore of Hector's chainsaw razzed the block as he lopped the limbs off a stubborn oak that had fallen against the house's freestanding clapboard garage. Ismael, meanwhile, busied himself in the yard, cramming the leftovers—dominoes, toy-wagon wheels, an ironing board, a lamp—into a black lawn bag he dragged behind him.

Directly across the street from us, a real estate agent and her subcontractor boyfriend had just finished cleaning out a foreclosure. Now ready for market, it would compete with the one we had just finished, as would the house next door, a new shotgun modular with a sale sign promising $895 DOWN BUYS THIS HOUSE NO BANK NEEDED.

The grass in the deacon's yard had filled out; it seemed to thrive despite the gallons of pesticide we'd dumped on it. Breezes played with the screen door, a rhythmic creak. Inside, not a scrap of paper was left: Ismael had cleaned the place out single-handedly. The only traces of the deacon that hadn't been stuffed into plastic bags were the names and phone numbers scribbled on the walls of the bathroom, the bedroom, the kitchen. The uncurtained windows made the place a little brighter. Even the carpet had been ripped out. Funny how the house showed a little promise now. My father didn't say much except to marvel at the tenacity of those fleas that remained. After taking a few pictures and locking up, he grabbed a can of repellent and sprayed his shoes. "Want some?" he offered.

I declined. But back in the truck, with Hillsborough Lane well behind us, the salsa music turned up, I felt a needling on my ankle. I lifted a pant leg, picked off the flea, and worried it between my fingernails, which were dirty and in bad need of a trimming but long enough, at least, to clip the vile pest.

And so I pinched, and saw just the slightest dab of blood.

THE DREAM
REVISITED

This is not the livelihood my father imagined for himself as a young man in Philadelphia, among the engineers and architects whose ranks he someday hoped to join, where he spent nearly every waking hour perfecting his draftsman's touch in Mylar and ink. Rather, foreclosures are one of several professional improvisations, slight reinventions set into motion by his exile from Cuba in 1962.

He landed in Miami at the age of fifteen with his younger brother, Tom (nine then), in tow. They grew up under the auspices of Jesuits, in a camp established by the archdiocese to help extract Cuban children from the influence of Communism, a mission known as Operation Pedro Pan. They lived in tents and barracks in what was still the rural outskirts of Miami—Opa-Locka, Homestead, and Florida City. Thousands of Cuban children came and went. Tom and my father were lucky: After promising not to separate them, the Jesuits couldn't find a family that would take them both. They became fixtures of the camp, matriculating through local schools. When my grandparents joined them in 1966, they all moved north to Philadelphia, where a cousin lived. There my father took the L to his gopher's job at United Engineers, then took the subway to night classes in engineering at Temple. He spent his lunch hours walking among the draftsmen's tables, tracing their blueprints, practicing while they gathered down the street at Dewey's, a greasy spoon. As luck would have it, an architect fell ill during deadline, and by then my father knew enough to finish the job. He upgraded. His American narrative was off to a good start.

With an architect's skills and an engineer's degree, he ventured into construction, a career that lasted most of my youth and led to several hometowns in the South: St. Petersburg in 1972, then Atlanta ('76), Rocky Mount, North Carolina ('80), then back to St. Petersburg again. With each move he tweaked his passion, so that drawing buildings led to building buildings, then building restaurants, until he had enough confidence to start his own construction company, which eventually buckled under the strain of a work-sapped marriage and poor accounting.

But with all the changes from town to town, he never strayed too far from construction. One could even argue that construction, in one form or another, contains a patrilineal thread for him, drawn from when his grandfather, a Spanish tycoon who'd made a fortune through the invention of a popular Cuban cracker, put him to work at the age of nine or so, laying block for a couple of rental units in Havana.

"When the plumbing broke," Dad told me, "my grandfather hired a plumber and gave me the tools and told the plumber to stand behind me and tell me what to do. Then there was this other guy, who worked the construction jobs my grandfather had. He was a laborer, digging ditches, laying block. His job was to teach me, you know, dig a ditch, how to lay a wall."

"You need to be taught how to dig a ditch?"

"Yes. I mean, it needs to be straight. There's a construction line—a *string* line—and how far you go this way for the footing, or that way, you need to make sure the block is straight."

It was during our Carolina phase that he tried to tie the patrilineal thread to me, partly to instill a work ethic, but more so as a way to spend some time together. Though I didn't know it at the time, our arrival in North Carolina was a bitter turning point in my parents' marriage. We'd been living in Atlanta, where my father worked for a family-diner empire called Sambo's. How that name could have seemed reasonable at all for an American business remains a mystery, but it worked, at least for a while, so that by the time my father joined them, Sambo's had over a thousand restaurants all over the West Coast and Southeast, with pancakes as the house specialty. At one point, Dad oversaw construction of every Sambo's east of the Mississippi, and can brag, I suppose, of having built 240 of them in a single year.

He still had some contextual gaps in his English, and didn't quite understand what kind of taboo the name was; but as these diners multiplied in the Northeast, the company caught hell. Nervous foremen would call my father from Weehawken and Manchester, New Hampshire, worried about the angry crowds that had begun to picket the corner. After a few years of this, and after other signs that Sambo's was on shaky ground, my father began to look elsewhere for work.

He answered a classified in the *Atlanta Constitution*, taken out by a company in Rocky Mount, North Carolina, called Boddie-Noell Enterprises. Among other things, they built Hardee's restaurants, through which they introduced a fast-food revolution: the breakfast biscuit. They were looking to blanket the Carolinas with as many Hardee's as they could fit into the fold, hopefully reaching into the Mid-Atlantic, then dipping into Tennessee. Lucrative work, a wide open future. Dad kept the appointment a secret from my mother, said only that his trip was work-related, and drove up to Rocky Mount for the interview.

About an hour south of Raleigh, Rocky Mount was a small town of forty thousand, and was known for little else other than a rivalry between barbecue clans (Gardner's drew the white crowd, Parker's the black) and, among jazz enthusiasts, as the birthplace of the great Thelonious Monk, who left before he ever formed a memory of the place.

The interview was a success. Afterward, Dad was invited to a company picnic on the Noell family plantation, a rolling twenty acres dotted with watering ponds, home to a black stud bull. The evening was a little balmy. Music layered over the open field. People danced half-drunk to doo-wop, buzzed around a pig turning on a spit. This turned out to be the first pig my father had tasted—the first pig he'd *seen*—since leaving Cuba. He nibbled on a rib, caught a sentimental vibe. A week or so later, when they offered him the job, he gladly accepted. Only then did he decide to share the good news with my mother.

She was a property manager at the time. After high school in Philadelphia, she'd gone to secretary school, then found a niche in real estate during our first stint in Florida. She got a real estate license to sell property, then a CPM to manage it, and wound up running a funky, six-story, argyle-patterned cube in St. Petersburg we called "the 300 Building," which still stands today in all its ugly Brutalist charm. The licenses were almost a matter of habit for her, a lover of tests; all told, she has real estate licenses from every state she's lived in—Florida, Georgia, North

Carolina, Texas—with the obscure CCIM (Certified Commercial Investment Member) in her arsenal of titles to boot.

In Atlanta, she worked as a real estate analyst for Metropolitan Life, poring over secondary mortgages they sought to purchase in bulk from various Savings and Loans. The Savings and Loan implosion left Metropolitan with more defaulted commercial property than it knew what to do with. My mother had the skills to step in, and took charge of a handful of properties for the company (one in Tampa, two in Louisville, another in Lexington). The authority, the travel, the responsibility, with a clientele to please and a staff to run—this was an empowering transformation for her at twenty-eight. So when my father broke the news that they'd be leaving cosmopolitan Atlanta so that he could take a job in what sounded like a backwater Carolina town, she threw a fit. Don't worry, he promised her, she'd love it. He drove her up to meet his bosses, their wives, see the plantation, tour a few neighborhoods where they might want to live. She threw an even bigger fit. Rocky Mount was slow suffocation compared to Atlanta—a *city*, for chrissakes, where they had *close friends* who *spoke Spanish*. She reeled, and in the last possible retaliation she could think of, held on in Atlanta after my father hauled me eight hours north. He and I moved into an apartment set behind the town's most beloved pizza parlor. I remember the racket the grackles made as they pasted our car with their acrid shit. My mother stayed behind as long as she could, metabolizing the indignity of this rude surprise, gnawing on the painfully problematic choice between a career—no small thing for a woman in the '70s, never mind an immigrant woman just a decade in the States—and us.

To persuade her, my father promised her a house.

He drew the plans himself, at the dinner table by night, an echo of his ambitions in Philadelphia. He found a calming solace in the precision of the slide rule, in every calculation, in the lead's straight and heavy lines, in what Le Corbusier called the "pure joy" of geometry. He drew a dream house, recalling whatever details he and my mother had admired in other homes, whatever touches she wanted that would articulate the perfect place to live.

She conceded, finally, angry but game—in short, devoted— and they spent their weekends driving around looking for the perfect lot, which they found in a rolling neighborhood on what was then the edge of town, then spent the next year watching as the house took form, stud by stud, pipe by pipe. The house was finished in the summer, one of several I spent in Florida with my mother's parents, so that I have two visions of the house in memory: the guts of its pine studs exposed, and done.

Built on an acre that sloped toward the street, the house was a shock to the faux-Colonial aesthetic all around it, low-slung and slotted into the rise like a Modernist ranch bunker with a cedar-shingled roof, each shingle hand cut to roughen up the light that played against it. Wide cedar steps rose along a subtle grade, winding toward the front door. Once inside, you walked into a wide open space, an interior vista that revealed a living room area set two feet down, the hallway acting as a kind of levee, and beyond that, sliding glass doors that framed the raised back deck and woods beyond—a Spanish courtyard of shifting elevations.

"There were a lot of houses for sale up there," he recalled when I asked him about this design, "but they were the traditional, colonial style. And I wanted to do something . . . Cuban. I wanted to do something from my background with a little bit of a different flavor to it."

"What made that house Cuban?" I asked him.

"Well, it wasn't Cuban. But it was . . . open . . . airy."

"Spanish."

"Not even that, just . . ."

"Modern."

"*Open.* I didn't want a formal dining room or family room or formal kitchen. That's why I took out the walls, so that there was a flow defined by either a drop in the floor or a rise of the ceiling. Not a physical divider, but visual. That house, when you came in, you knew you were in the living room, either by the use of materials, by utilization of the volume, or the floor elevation, but there was no wall. In fact, when I was building it, people would go there and they'd say, 'You going to put a rail here?' And I'd say, 'No way. If you fall two feet, you fall two feet.' I wanted it so that when you walked in, you were slightly higher, you felt like the master of the space."

To the right, toward the kitchen, a set of steps led deeper than the living room down into a spot we called the Conversation Pit, a hot décor touch of the decade. It was a plush pit, with a sofa built into one end and a fireplace on the other, set into a wall of shelves that ran floor to ceiling, Pit to ceiling, eighteen feet. Glancing left from the entrance, a bright pine staircase corkscrewed up into an enormous finished attic, where the TV was, where my father's office was. Past that staircase, the levee became a formal hallway, with bedrooms opening along either side, shotgun style.

All of us—my father, my mother, and I—still discuss that house with great affection. Not all our memories of it are nostalgic; as my father grew increasingly obsessed with work, he spent less time in the home he built, until my mother's anger over leaving Atlanta warped into an even deeper sadness, magnified by all that square footage. But while sadness colors it, the house still shimmers in my memory as a work of art. Even as a boy I could sense the talent it revealed in my father, recognizing, for the first time, not only his ability to build something, but an imagination at work—and better, a brilliance. So I was proud to live there, even then. And ever since our sudden, tail-between-the-legs departure from that town, after my father was let go by the company that brought us to Rocky Mount, this house has loomed like a moody temple in my imagination, beautiful but inextricably linked to our unraveling, and to the shame of losing it to another family. "Sold quick," my father remembers, "because it was so different. The first guy who saw it." And the temple looms, set back in that piney lot, large and complicated in my imagination; which is why, years ago, I salvaged the blueprints from his Tampa attic, and have kept them since, so that someday, with enough time and money, I might build that house again, start over, and raise a family there.

Dad was a workaholic before we knew what to call it. He binged on paperwork during the week, and on weekends cruised all over the Carolinas to inspect the Hardee's sites under his charge—new projects and remodeling jobs in towns smaller than ours, where a Hardee's grand opening drew a pretty good crowd, and where each became an outpost of social life. He regretted all the time he spent away from my mother and me in Atlanta, but was no less busy now. His solution was to combine devotions, consolidate by bringing us with him on weekend inspections. This was his awkward way of bonding: We didn't play sports, we didn't fish. We went to Hardee's.

You can bet it was miserable. Think of all the sunlit days I would have rather spent burning something, or riding a bike.

Instead, I watched the Carolinas roll past, or stretched out in the backseat to read a book. We chatted, of course, but neither of us remember the details of those conversations. We have only visceral memories of different moods.

The ritual involved some deceit. Dad would ask me to come along with him for a short ride, an errand, and we would run that errand, but then continue out of town toward Tarboro or Wilson, about ten, twenty miles away. I'd watch him converse with strangers and point and tell others what to do. If the Hardee's in question was open, we'd eat there; if it was still under construction, we'd stop and eat at one on the way. Two stops, then a third, as many as five. They became all-day affairs, dull patrols. The day seemed elastic. There was only so much fast food I could eat.

The trips stretched to Virginia (Roanoke, Petersburg, Thomasville) and east to Carrboro. Just getting near the car with him was a risk. The sounds of his preparation—the click of pens and pencils, rustling through his briefcase, the trill and snap of a rubber band on rolled-up blueprints—all announced a road trip, and made me nervous. I'd hear him warming up, and find a corner of the house to avoid him. Or I would refuse. But each time he promised the trip would be short, and fun, and would outwit me; or he would plead; or he'd simply demand that I come in a tone that erased any choice. Mostly, though, he preferred the ruse, and I remember his laugh, which sprung the moment I'd realize—seeing Highway 64 in the near distance, or seeing, too late, that we'd glided onto a stretch of road along which the signs of town were thinning—that I'd been duped into another long trip. I'd moan, and he'd laugh at my finally being in on the joke.

He felt grounded in this ritual. It reminded him of his own

youth, when his grandfather put him to work at the bakery, or helping to build the rental: carrying tiles for the roofers, pushing a wheelbarrow of trash, stacking bricks, digging the ditch. He idolized his grandfather, and was thrilled to impress him, but that legacy in construction would have to wait with me. These were, after all, commercial sites, and the foremen would have thought my father was nuts if he'd handed me a hammer and set me loose. Instead I snooped, darted through unfinished walls and studied the ductwork, the electrical guts. I dodged the carpenters. I fiddled with sawdust and odd, lopped corners of two-by-fours. At first the noise of these sites was a horror, the pace too hectic. But I got used to it, so that the hammering and shrieks of saws sounded less like clatter and more like a familiar song.

I eventually sought refuge from the trips through my mother, but that didn't work; my father simply brought her with us. She had trouble refusing, since the day-to-day in town had so little to offer. After leaving her job in Atlanta, she had trouble finding work in Rocky Mount. Among middle-class women there, housewifery was the thing. She tried to follow suit, killing time with racquetball lessons, accounting classes, shopping, decorating the house my father built her, that extravagant penance. But mainly, for her, those exercises paled next to actual work, and filled her days instead with a boredom profound enough that it likely touched existential edges. So any excuse to get out was a relief.

I've often turned to my parents to help me rummage through the details of our lives in Rocky Mount, because my own memory feels so weak on the subject. To listen to them is to try and balance two emotional truths. My father remembers Rocky Mount more fondly, mainly because of our trips; he also possesses a talent for gently refusing regret—or, at least, internalizing it. My mother, meanwhile, though demure, is more blunt ("Boring doesn't describe it."). As far as she's concerned, that town was five years wasted. So while my father recalls those years with an easy warmth, there's a thunder off at a short count in my mother's telling. The result is a confusion of loyalty. Choosing an attitude toward my Carolina childhood is, in a way, choosing sides.

I finally got the chance to work for my father the summer I turned fourteen, our first full summer back in Florida. Hardee's was behind us by then, and my father had just started his own construction company. My first job for him—my first job ever—was what he described as a bit of demolition work at a Wendy's on the beach. I expected sweet rewards from this gig: the serenity of the Gulf in summer, girls walking past and catching glances, and the pride in telling others that I, just a skinny kid, worked in construction.

The Wendy's was close to water, but about a mile from an actual beach, on the landlocked side of a bridge that crossed an inlet. Yes, we saw girls, but only as they drove past. The site itself was a disaster: arson. And while the fire never actually left the kitchen, every inch of drop ceiling had been blackened by the smoke. Water was everywhere—a foot deep in the kitchen, dripping from dangling pipes and pieces of hanging metal, and oozing from the carpet in the dining room, black with soot. A hole in the kitchen ceiling provided the only light, the only air through which the building vented a thick, humid stink of burned metal, burned grease, burned wood, and burned plastic. The grease in the deep fryers hadn't even cooled enough to congeal. Every breathable cubic inch of the place was toxic. And I was lured in, imagining the beach, and instead, for two weeks, a friend and I hauled the place apart piece by piece. We grabbed anything in the kitchen that could be moved and tore loose what was stubborn and eventually dragged it all out, I don't know how many tons of it, to be tossed into a rented Dumpster out back. We tore out every inch of carpet, removed every ceiling panel. We performed, in essence, a surgical demolition, after which the interior of the Wendy's would be rebuilt. My father calculated that this would be cheaper than bulldozing the place and starting over. It seemed like an awesome impossibility, like bailing out the blasted guts of a sinking ship. But in a month the Wendy's opened again, and from then on I could brag, I suppose, about my first work-related injury, a nail through the foot.

The next year, I had a chance to avoid construction altogether when my father surprised me with a job at a nearby Burger King. He'd remodeled the place, and had gotten the manager to agree to hire me. My father introduced us while we were on an errand, the job was already mine. Backing out would have embarrassed him; the marriage had been arranged.

What I saved in sweat I suffered in humiliation, as anyone who has worn that shackling polyester while serving the hungry and impatient can attest. The job made you uglier. The steaming vats were a primer for some glandular malfunction; the uniform itself seemed designed to spread pimples. The cooks were angry, the drive-through frenetic. The whole place had the spirit of a jailbreak.

This job was too painful. I quit after two weeks, but not before making one friend, Laminka, who shared her breaktime with me, and about whom the most vivid detail I've kept is the alarming amount of ketchup she dumped on her fries—two

handfuls of packets. It seemed like vengeance for her, a retaliation against our poor wages.

I also made an enemy, a long-haired boy whose final gesture
was to request a fight. A coworker relayed the details: I was supposed to return the next day, when the angry one was working,
and meet him by the Dumpster. I only remember the green uniform of the messenger, not even his face. "But this is my last
day," I told him. "Right," he said, sympathetically, "but he wants
you to come back tomorrow, anyway, after his shift, and then he
can fight you." I had missed some important code here. I laughed,
baffled. The messenger shrugged. In piecing this together,
though, I think I've figured out the motive: My father had gotten me the job through his connection to the manager, which
automatically made me a pet; but worse, I didn't own a car then,
and would often borrow my father's shining, white BMW 635 to
drive to work. This car had appeared just after my mother had
divorced him, had helped him rally against the midlife crisis
the divorce had triggered. Meanwhile, I looked ridiculous driving it, never mind driving it to work at Burger King, which the
others must have thought was some cruel comment on how dis-
pensable the job actually was. In retrospect the logic seems
simple: bird-boned, pimply boy, in full Burger King uniform
and visor, pulls up in a gleaming, German-engineered chick
magnet, a muscle car with a nose like a Learjet, bright white, and
kills a few hours working the drive-through. There was enough
absurdity in this that even I would want to beat me up.

That winter my father and I worked our last fast-food job
together. Our proudest, in fact, again a Wendy's. We had no
more than a night—between when the place shut down at nine
to when it opened the next morning, just before lunch—to remove
a wall and replace it with a salad bar, that fast-food revolution of

the late '80s. Cousins from Colombia were in town and helped out. The job was a hyperactive family affair. Any customer who was the last to leave Wendy's that night, and loyal enough to return for lunch the next day, would have seen a magical transformation: Out went the eight-foot, oak-and-stained-glass divider, and, with the power of jackhammers and torches and a dozen hands, in went the future: salad!

By now, as far as I can tell, all those salad bars have disappeared.

For every dozen or so notices we taped to a door or slipped inside a mailbox—guessing a soon-to-be-foreclosed home might be occupied but not willing to linger long enough to find out—we took our chances and knocked. Late one day, after hours of driving, we approached a house just off I-275, in a neighborhood of cruddy single stories with gutted cars in the yard and enclosed patios, their screens ratty and casting an eerie shade. An ice-cream truck rolled through the neighborhood, squeezing a tinny reggaetón ditty through the megaphone on its roof. Country boys leaned against a jacked-up diesel pickup, chatting. Perhaps it was the dismissiveness with which they told my father that someone still lived in the house next door; whatever it was, he decided it was safe to knock. He went up to the screen door and tapped it. A woman's voice, big and rough, boomed from inside. She came to the door in purple scrubs.

The exchange was brusque but not tense, and when my father mentioned the bank, she mentioned Eddie, that we were probably looking for him. My father gave her Mena's number, they thanked each other, and we assumed by her presence and Eddie's absence that an illness was the cause of his predicament. "But see," my father said, turning around at a dead end, driving past the house again, "how did he get a mortgage on *that* house? That house doesn't pass FHA. It doesn't pass a lot of criteria."

"It's a piece of junk," I said.

"Subprime," my father said. "I'll bet he couldn't go anywhere to get a decent loan. A guy probably promised him a loan but said there's no way the bank would do it. So he gets a loan at thirteen percent, five points."

Weeks went by before Eddie called, and it wasn't until I heard the nurse's voice again, bleating through a speakerphone in Mena's home office, that the facts were parceled out. The nurse, Gwen, had lived in the house for ten years, but somehow Eddie owned it, and had refinanced it, and had lost it. Both she and Eddie were on the line, confused about Mena's explanation of the foreclosure process, and even more confused by the cash-for-keys offer. And underneath their confusion was an undeniable desperation to keep the house.

Eddie had tried to cover the risk of an adjustable-rate loan through refinancing that finally caught up with him. He was vague with the numbers and spat out the names of the banks he'd dealt with—Ameriquest, Wells Fargo, et al.

Gwen interrupted: "We been trying to finance, and we wish we could find somebody to finance so we won't have to move."

"I'm sorry about this," Mena said, "but this is already, you know, done. The bank already closed. The bank is the owner now. And, unfortunately, you know, you guys don't have any other option but to accept the cash for keys or be evicted."

I could hear Eddie moaning on the other end of the line.

"Is there no way that we can move out and then try to rebuy the house back again?" Gwen asked.

"The only way that you might be able to buy the house back is maybe have your family purchase the house and, later on, they can do a deed to you, and you can be the owner. But if you had a hard time trying to get somebody to refinance the house, it's going to be more difficult now, because automatically your credit score dropped two hundred points."

We couldn't figure out if the noises coming over the line were speakerphone glitches or noises of distress—voices broken, vowels dragging.

"So I'm sorry there aren't other solutions. Just trying to do the best on getting all the stuff together so you can move, you know. But as I mentioned before, the condition with the cash-for-keys is that the house needs to be free of all debris. Do you have a lot of stuff?"

"Yeah. It'll take more than two weeks."

"Well, see, you told me you want two thousand dollars and you'd be out in two weeks. But now you're telling me that you're not sure you're going to be out in two weeks."

"We supposed—I don't want no eviction notice," Gwen said, pleading. "You know, I got enough pride in myself, I don't want to go evicted. I don't want to go out like, you know, somebody comin' in and the sheriff comin' up here and stuff like that. I been livin' in this neighborhood for *ten years* and never had a problem. I want to go out in class. I wanted to stay here. It's breakin' my heart, you know. You know?"

It occurred to Mena that Gwen had never been listed on any of the paperwork for the house—not the deed, not a single one of Eddie's attempts at refinancing—and that, since her name had stayed off the books, her lack of credit history was their only chance. Gwen could, in theory, qualify for a loan that would allow her to buy the house after it went back on the market. She brought home $1,400 a month. Mena guessed the house was now worth about $80,000, "which would make your payments around $1,000 a month. Can you afford that?"

Gwen burst out, "Yes, ma'am, we'll do it! Yes, ma'am! Yes, ma'am! We'll do it! Won't miss a damn payment. You don't have to worry about it, the thousand dollars will be there every month—*every month.* I don't want to move from this house, ma'am. I will do anything. The bank will get their thousand dollars every month. *On time.*"

It wasn't an offer, it was a scenario, and Mena spent the next several minutes explaining that the house was already gone, but that, without making any promises, she would ask if the bank would be willing to postpone the eviction while Gwen sought financing to buy the house herself. "Don't put Eddie on the loan," Mena reminded her. "Eddie, you're on the blacklist now."

I left the room and stepped outside for a minute, over-whelmed, knowing we'd likely see Gwen and Eddie again, with a sheriff's deputy in front of us. Even if Gwen could get a loan, there wasn't a single institution that would lend her a cent for that shabby house. Hearing Gwen's panicked voice, I began to understand the depth and pain of the crisis in a way that burned a hole through all the financial analysis, a voice and emotion that often remained conveniently muted behind the junk. And while there were those who knew what they'd gotten themselves into, who were prepared to take the financial hit and walk away, and others scrambling to protect what they could through the maddening paperwork of bankruptcy, sniffing for loopholes, and others still who went about their daily motions thousands of miles away from the loss, there were those, like Gwen, who seemed trapped in pathetic confusion, having been misled by their own desire, taught as a tenet of good citizenship in America, to own something permanent; in this case, a house that was now practically worthless, that merely marked a spot for bulldozers when it came time to widen the interstate.

E ven after the dissolution of Bear Stearns, there was hesita-
tion among financial pundits to make comparisons between
this crisis and the Great Depression. But by September 2008,
with the collapse of Lehman Brothers and the meltdowns of
both Fannie Mae and Freddie Mac, the doomsayers had a lot
more room to stretch. The economic knot of toxic mortgages,
unemployment, and frozen credit had grown large enough to
swallow a pair of Wall Street juggernauts. Among voters during
that year's presidential election, the crisis had easily surpassed
the Iraq War as their most grievous concern. John McCain
pandered to that anxiety, suspending his campaign to attend
brainstorming sessions on the Treasury's corporate-bailout
plan, hoping, it seemed, for some legislative heroics. But he was
a war candidate appealing to a crowd plagued with genuine economic fear.

The housing crisis threatened to turn exaggeration into
prediction. Even the visual aids were dramatic: the graphs were
steep, the front pages splashed with what by then had become a

visual refrain of stockbrokers guffawing skyward in disbelief. That image was already a clichéd visual aid of the business pages; the difference now was that guffawing was being done not only by traders on Wall Street, but slack-jawed traders in Europe, Asia, and India.

The economic shock triggered grave comparisons, and the benchmark quickly reached past 2002, past Black Monday '87, past references to the Carter administration and gas lines, and began to settle, finally, with World War II and the Great Depression. By the time Barack Obama won the presidential election, hyperbole had lost its juice. Even the timing of the stock market's plummet in early October (2,268 points, 22 percent, in just seven trading days) seemed to suggest an autumnal tradition, as if stock market plunges were timed with the equinox. The Dow would hit a low on March 9, 2009, of 6,547 points, not seen in more than a decade, with a decade's wealth wiped out.

The Obama administration crafted a calculated resonance with Franklin Roosevelt's New Deal initiatives, calling for a Green New Deal. His inauguration speech was sober and vigilant, absent of any single mantra we could fold into memory. Just weeks into his presidency, the historical knot would be officially sewn together when Obama himself, in his first prime-time news conference, would refer to this as "the worst economic crisis since the Great Depression"—a claim he made as a candidate, but which, now that he was president, carried an entirely new weight. Soup kitchens were beginning to strain; homeless shelters were taking in more and more of the recently dispossessed, from different classes; and suicides, while isolated, still crept into the news as a measure of comparison. The Great Depression remained exponentially worse, but it was the last benchmark left.

On Election Day, many of the placards advertising homes for sale and calls for help had been removed by city workers, replaced with flocks of political pickets jammed into the grass by volunteers. Along with the official signage for the presidential campaigns, there was the handmade stuff: FOR SALE and FOR RENT signs that had been snuck into place; NO OBAMA, NO HUS-SEIN signs; pickets for tax collectors seeking your vote, for con-gressman, for yard sales. Signs for CHANGE. Signs beseeching we vote YES ON 2.

I spent Election Day driving around looking for a scandal. In the weeks leading up to November 4, I'd kept up with reports on the potential impact of "foreclosure lists" at the polls. The sus-picion among Obama supporters was that the majority of fore-closure victims would, because of their demographic profile (minorities, the lower-middle-class), vote for Obama, and that, because of this trend, GOP poll watchers would use lists of fore-closure victims to compare addresses. If a voter's address given at the poll on Election Day matched their address on the fore-closure list, they'd have trouble voting, since technically they no longer resided at that foreclosed address; similarly, if someone's address on their driver's license didn't match the address where they'd ended up (because of being foreclosed upon, for example), that inconsistency would also stymie the process. Those voters would get to vote eventually, through provisional ballots, but the fear was that such complications would interfere with—if not discourage altogether—the act of voting.

But Election Day was quiet. Gray and damp and cool. Read-ing weather. In St. Petersburg, poll workers looked placid, if not bored, idling at the doorways on cigarette breaks. Early voting had absorbed potential logjams at most stations. In Tampa, there were lines, and one poll was backed up well into the night, but for the most part the controversies were limited to rudeness and a lot of waiting, both complaints being reported after the election had been won.

At home, flipping among the channels, searching for some sign of the drama we'd come to expect, my father shook his head at all that blue, and didn't hide his displeasure.

"Jimmy Carter Number Two," he said.

"It's beautiful," I gloated.

"Just wait," he said. "Think interest rates are high now? Wait. You were a little baby when I was paying eighteen percent and gas lines were two blocks long. Just wait."

THE next day, a familiar drill, this time on Emma Street, to check and see if a home is occupied or empty, switch the locks, take a few pictures, slap a lockbox on the door, and move on. The house had been sitting idle for a while but had finally made it to the top of someone's stack of paperwork. The time had come to try and get it off the books.

Emma Street is a straight shot of several blocks' worth of single-story duplexes and humble bungalows about a decade old, small, with touches of retro-historic flair like Doric-columned porticos, the columns not quite proportional to the modest size of the house. These were flanked by ranch homes—some a taupe stucco, others brick, each house painted a cheerful color. Some fences looked stronger than others, some landscaping more alive than the rest. Half the driveways were made of sand. The windows of one columned bungalow were slapped over with plywood. Tennis shoes hung every block or so from the telephone lines above the street, like deflated dirty lanterns from a long-dead festival. Just a few blocks up, the street simply ended where it met the railroad tracks, then began again on the other side. The city hadn't even bothered to complete the street, leaving it a dead end on both sides.

I'd brought the monkey wrench from the truck's toolbox, but coming up the driveway, into the carport, we found the side door cracked open. Dad walked in first, gently pushing, and a thick stench of piss and mold wafted over us, which meant something was open somewhere else inside, a breeze passing through. We walked inside. The odor wrapped around us, strong enough that it almost had a texture to it. Clothes were scattered toward the corners, in a gray light smothered by the blinds. Dad's back was stiff, and he kind of waddled down the darkened hall toward the bedrooms. I heard my father's knuckle tap and push the back bedroom door open. I leaned and watched him peek into the black. He glanced at the floor, twitched, then leaned back just a little. He sang a very harmless "hello," as if greeting a child.

"What's up." The voice had been sleeping, but even groggy, and disembodied, it boomed, and seeped into the hallway a little, and was big enough that you didn't necessarily want to see the body attached to it. The empty room amplified the fella's size, maybe. But already the voice projected an outline there in the dark: black, middle-aged, sluggish. I saw the plaid back of my father's shirt against the black of the room, and leaned in to see a sliver of light that cut between the window and the wad of insulation that had been shoved into it, for shade.

"Y'all the bank?"

"We're here to . . ." and my father trailed off, hoping he'd get it.

"All right," he said.

"You live here?"

"Yessir," he said, a Southern touch. He struggled to get up.

"Okay," Dad said. "That's all right. Take your time."

"All right."

Dad seemed surprised but not scared. Both he and the voice were gentle with each other.

"How ya'll doin' this morning?" he asked us.

"All right," Dad said. "Take your time, take your time."

I could hear the fellow getting dressed, the shuffle of him putting his pants on, the click of a belt. I leaned in just a little and saw his leg and a white sock, and the mattress on the floor, and the dust motes creeping through the light the insulation let pass.

He stepped out into the hallway. He was tall and thin and, closer to the light, showed hard years on him. "You look at the election last night?" he asked us.

My father didn't understand him.

"You look at the election last night?"

"Oh! Yep!" Dad said. "It was good, eh?"

The voice nodded with grainy smile. "Yeah." He hesitated by the bathroom door, a little shy. "I gotta get a little something and then I'll get out your way."

He retreated into the bathroom and locked the door, and we went back outside and left him in peace. We both breathed in deep, partly for the tension but also because the air was finally more breatheable. On the front doorknob, a flyer dangled from the knob, between the screen and front doors: VOTE OBAMA TUES NOV 4. POLLS ARE OPEN. There was something absurd but admirably complete in the gesture, of opening that first door and slipping this thing onto the knob, and who knows if it occurred to whomever had volunteered to canvass these blocks if it did any good, of how many of these doorknob flyers dangled from doors of empty houses, or houses wherein the invisible and disenfranchised and likely unvoting would return to at night.

Birds chirped. Dad tried to bend and stretch a little. We could hear the wash of traffic. My father looked brittle. There was nothing to do but wait until the man inside came out, so we just kicked the leaves and chatted.

He asked me to get a Phillips screwdriver from the truck's toolbox, but all I could find was a massive flathead. He dug through the clinking junk himself.

"Think he's squatting?"

"Could be." He kept digging, pausing, digging. "I need a Phillips longer than this," he said. "The guys use my screwdrivers and don't give them back." He had about a dozen flatheads now, but no Phillips, and he stepped around to the other side, frustrated.

I found the Phillips. My father pointed to the far end of the yard. The man we'd found had rolled out from behind the other side of the house on a frail-looking bicycle, wobbling slowly across the grass until he bounced onto the street, still wobbling, pedaling slowly, not in any hurry, but not looking back.

We didn't get the trash-out on Emma Street at first. The request from the bank was simply to change the locks. The trash-out was instead assigned to Field Asset Services, one of a handful of national companies that handled what was known as "mortgage field services," newspeak for trash-outs and lawn mowing and the like, the same work we did, but managed through a corporate structure. Lately, banks had been hiring these companies as a one-stop-shopping source for cleaning up and maintaining foreclosures, which in theory was supposed to have made expediting them more efficient. But in the case of the house on Emma, FAS never sent anyone—or, if they did, whoever showed up saw what it took to clean it and refused. The house sat idle; squatters came and went. Six months later, Hector and Ismael descended upon it. This would happen time and again: handymen and landscapers signing up online, getting a call, or an e-mail, then walking into scenarios and neighborhoods they hadn't anticipated, which in some cases scared them enough that, after months of back-and-forth between Mena and the bank—with Mena never actually getting to speak directly to the people FAS had hired—the job would sit, and sit, until finally the bank asked her to get it done.

Work was scattered for Hector and Ismael all that fall. It would remain scattered all through winter, too, and into spring, for a good year or so. My father assigned them odd jobs and repairs around the house, any excuse to put them to work. They had become, over the last decade and a half, limited by their specialization. Neither spoke English well enough, or spoke it confidently enough, to hustle around for jobs much better than this one. By working for my father, the two of them had arguably found the career best suited to their talents. Manual labor is manual labor, but this job was strange enough to take stories home. Even Mr. Lopez, who normally mowed and weeded the lawns of Mena's foreclosures, wasn't working as much. The lawns were in the hands of field servicers based in Dallas. And despite all the taxpayer money that was filtering through the banks and into the coffers of Safeguard Properties and FAS, the lawns were growing, the houses sitting vacant and vulnerable.

The field servicers made sense in theory: Rather than receive hundreds of invoices from dozens of agents who hired the handymen in their Rolodexes, a field service company maintained a network of contractors in dozens of cities. The field service company created a pay scale depending on the job and, depending on the list of repairs an agent submitted to the bank, would assign tasks from that list, collect invoices for work done in a particular county or city, then add up the cost and charge the bank a single fee—padded, of course, for the cost and convenience of reducing the bank's own paperwork. In this way, it was assumed that the agent would be liberated from the upkeep of a foreclosure, so that they could focus on selling the property instead.

Indeed, the paperwork was reduced, but the work itself could be sloppy, with trash-outs left unfinished. Mena often discovered at least another half-day's worth of work before a foreclosure was in good enough shape to sell, which created its own round of e-mails, more days of waiting for approval, and hiring Hector and Ismael to finish the job. What's more, the field servicers were driving down the cost of labor among the subcontractors they hired, so that a re-key that once cost twenty-five bucks was paying only fifteen or so, while the servicer still charged fifty bucks on the other end. This was a proven formula for profit-making but, given that it kept costs high for the banks, it was a formula that succeeded at the taxpayer's and laborer's expense. The banks could argue that different arms of its operations were responsible for different expenditures, losses, profits, and the like, but in essence, when all was said and done, it was TARP money that helped keep companies like Safeguard and FAS in the black.

Then again, the same could be said for the work we did. Except that now, more often than not, the work was going to handymen who did a worse job than Hector and Ismael but who somehow had connected with the big-box servicers. And when I finally did register on FAS's Website, and follow up by calling one of its regional service managers, the only response I got was, "Naw, we straight in Florida."

We were witnessing the growing pains of an industry—or, at least, the exponential growth of what was once a niche, the acceleration of a job that once skulked along the margins of the housing market into a major industry being quickly consolidated—without any regulation, by a handful of companies with excellent corporate and political ties. It was an all-American path.

"I have a house here in *Town & Country*," Mena told me, by way of example. "They don't have me take care of the grass, they don't have me be in charge of cleaning it. I'm supposed to just put up the for-sale sign. Once in a while I'll drive by the house, and the grass is high. Because these vendors are based in Dallas, or they have an office in Jacksonville. But they don't send a guy from Jacksonville to do *one* job, they wait until there are *ten* properties to deal with. I keep an eye on those properties. I send an e-mail to the bank telling them the property looks bad. I take a photo. The field servicers say they're supposed to take care of it, and the bank's pressuring me about why the house hasn't sold, but this house looks *terrible*, and it's *overpriced*, and no one's cutting the grass! So what happened? We got a citation from the homeowners association. I said, 'Bingo!' Then Nationstar calls and says, 'Mena, give me an estimate.' So your dad puts together an estimate, and he finished the job."

"We do it right," Dad said as he walked into the room. "And we do it economically."

"It would be awkward if Safeguard was cheaper," Mena said. "But they're not—*and* they do a lousy job."

"Lousy," Dad said. "On the remodels, you should see the carpet they're using. They're even leaving the old pad! And I *never* do that, because a pad smells. I always remove the old tack-strips, I put down a six-pound pad, nice carpet. You should see— let me show you the carpet." He turned and went into the other room to get the sample, then brought back a beige square, tough as a scouring pad.

"Let me show you the one I'm using," he said, and went and fetched it, and held the two together. It was the same color, more or less, and the same weave—a berber—but not as tightly wound, not as tough. And the difference may have been subtle, but it was important, since the idea is to make the house, in all its aspects, no matter the neighborhood, attractive, and Mena saw little hope in winning over buyers whose short list of fix-ups included replacing all the carpet. "And the same pad!" he said again. "The one I took a picture of in Oldsmar that those guys put in? It had cat piss on it!"

———

Later that week I checked in on Joe Koebel. He'd just received a house after it had been taken away from an agent who'd had trouble selling it. Joe's inventory had nearly doubled since I'd last seen him—from thirty-five to sixty houses. "They all sold," he said, hunched over at one of a cluster of computer terminals packed into a room that connected parallel hallways. "But they keep coming."

He slid away from the computer. "The paper the other day, there was an article where the guy has got four or five vacant houses in the neighborhood, and he's mowing their lawns for nothing, just to keep up appearances. There was a lady this morning—you read it this morning? The lady who lives on fifty acres? She's got, like, thirty vacant lots right by her house that she just bought."

I'd seen it. The *St. Petersburg Times* had discovered a mother of five named Angie Harris in a subdivision that had already made the pages of the *Tampa Tribune* that summer, wherein a handful of homeowners lived scattered among the ninety acres of a development interrupted called Tanglewood Preserve. It would become a kind of poster village of the middle-class fore-closure crisis, a few months later, when *The New Yorker* reported on Harris and her neighbors. They lived in what was known as a "ghost subdivision," and over the next year or so its portrait would become as ubiquitous as the shell-shocked traders staring upward in disbelief from the trading floor.

Harris and her husband, a U.S. Navy intelligence officer who'd been sent to Bahrain, bought their home in July for a hundred thousand less than the asking price. They knew the risks—the evidence was all around them—but assumed houses would follow when the market recovered, a prognosis of a year at most. Now the lots were thick and weedy, used as dumps. But the streets were paved, with charming names. The same was pretty much true for tens of thousands of lots within an hour's radius: sewer, power, but still waiting for the house.

"I just sold a house down in Riverview," Koebel said. "Same thing. Built in 2005–06. Going into it, you go by a school, and then there's just rows and rows and rows of streets of vacant lots. It's just bare land with stakes in the ground. The builder couldn't make the payments. That was the end of that."

The pressure had lessened only slightly since I'd last seen him. "I knew it was going to get worse," he said. "I haven't had a day off. I'm doing re-keys, BPOs, the monthlies. I been working till nine at night. I have no life. I just stuck in five grand of my own money to take care of water and power bills in deposits for the foreclosures I've got. Five grand in a week!" The banks covered it, of course, but on a sixty-to-ninety-day payout, which meant that any agent with poor cash flow who took on these properties could easily become buried by the costs of keeping them up themselves. Koebel wiggled his can to feel if there was any soda left. "I'm screwed if the banks collapse and don't pay me," he said.

With such an overwhelming number of houses coming online, why not turn a few down? It seemed a reasonable, if not precautious, solution.

"I hate turning it down," he said. "I went so many years without getting any business." His solution was to make his wife, Monica, spend more time with him at the office helping to process paperwork, and to hire an old colleague who was having trouble selling traditional houses, a behemoth of a man named Jesse— six-four, frame of a pulling guard, with a permanently non- plussed demeanor.

"Some nights," Joe told me, picking up on the litany of his suffering, "the vein on the side of my neck was throbbing. I was becoming a robot. I couldn't take it anymore." He shook his empty diet cola again and stared at the greaseboard. There was as much green as red, though that didn't seem to ease his worry.

Thanksgiving approached, with none of autumn's flashes. The flora here sheds invisibly. Still, November days in the subtropics are a strong second to New England's October turning. The air is lighter by now, cooler and finally a little dry, but still warm under the sun. November is the prelude to the Florida winter that made this place a mecca for consumptives and Canadians. For the snowbird, the Florida winter is a still-life of the Indian summers back home, an extended lease on autumn's sense of expectation, of life turning a corner, but without the misery of a sooty freeze. As far as freezes go, except for a handful in a century, the odds are in your favor against it.

I was on a Sunday drive, on MLK (still Buffalo Avenue on some maps) looking for the turn to Deacon Logan's church. The sky was a cosmic blue, brushed clean by a cold front. I knew where Logan worshipped—First Born Church of the Living God—and ever since his phone had gone out, I knew the only way to reach him would be to crash a service, which I dreaded doing. I am a very lapsed Catholic, more inclined to believe that

Jesus was an theocratic activist than the son of God. Church tends to make me restless, and rituals beyond that, nervous. The more fervent the faith, the more nervous I get. The evangelical style is beyond me, the Pentecostal off the grid altogether. In a tie or in a burka, a zealot is a zealot.

Judging by what the deacon told me, First Born Church of the Living God sounded like a humble, black evangelical church in a poor black neighborhood, which meant that even with the holy-day mood on my side, I would be an interruption, the only white man in the room catching stares of suspicion. I would be an interloper draped in a satchel full of gear, taking notes. But with Logan's number out of service, I wanted to find him before he disappeared altogether.

The neighborhood was quiet. CHANGE pickets left over from the election stood in a few front yards. Some were crooked, some straight, and all were, this long after the election, beginning to resonate with something other than the victory they implied. I never saw one in a neighborhood that wasn't poor. The longer they stayed up, the more they spoke to a longer arc of history. The pickets would winnow in number over the following months, tossed away or ripped out by the weather. But the ones that remained, sticking out in front yards here and there, seemed to inject a strange subtext to the growing distance between the euphoria of November and the pain of the unfolding months. After a while, the picket's inspirational message seemed more like a private matter. The zeitgeist faded much more quickly than I'd expected. Even for the pickets we gathered at trash-outs, the ironic context had disappeared: just another historical scrap swept up in the moody archaeology of the job.

I turned on Thirtieth Avenue. Children huddled in an unshaded backyard for Sunday school, and as I turned, none turned to look at who was driving past. They were focused. Down the street, elders strolled in suits and bright, elaborate dresses. The avenue was flanked by shotgun shacks, a meat market, Leon's Cut Rate Package Liquor, Juancho's Place, and finally First Born Church, with a handful of cars parked in a sandy lot.

I could hear the pastor's voice humming through the cranked-up system inside. I was late. I looked for a side door, an office entrance, and a drained-looking dude appeared from around the corner of the building. "Trying to get to church?" he said.

"I'm looking for a side office. I don't want to interrupt."

"Ain't no side office," he said. "You can go up through *that* door—everybody else goes through that door."

The only thing worse than being late for church is being late to a church you don't even belong to, and being stared at as you enter. I swallowed and walked in, saw that the foyer was enclosed, and that the choice was between entering on the right or left side. I chose right, entered the small room, and met the glances of the pastor and the elders around him. I slipped as quickly as I could into a pew.

Pastor Jeremiah Cook was in full stride, a hoarse-throated homily. His voice shoved itself through brittle speakers set in the corner of the room. He saw me but didn't miss a beat. Others turned but only glanced. I'd slipped into the last pew, behind a family of three—mother, father, and a toddler boy. The boy noticed me. He was restless, delighted for the interruption. The couple traded him back and forth, holding him and bouncing him and giving him a toy car or the Bible to chew on or whatever they could find to occupy him and keep him quiet, and somehow always focused on Pastor Cook—listening and nodding and passing the boy between them.

Pastor Cook was flanked by two men in suits—one young, one an elder. They punctuated the emotional logic of his message with hands flying up, a palm to the congregation, a palm to the heavens, with shouts of affirmation tumbling over the arrhythmic chorus of the families seated in the pews across the aisle, who moaned and chirped and rocked, girls and grandmothers and all.

Deacon Logan was sitting up front in a pew that faced the pulpit, alone, nodding and mulling over the homily. Then he looked at me, with a stare that pushed the couple in front of me aside, that same peering look he had when I met him in the spring: between a scowl and searching, as if hurt by something I'd said. His eyes tightened, and he didn't smile.

Pastor Cook barreled on, with other voices filling in the pauses: "God says, 'You got a relationship with your wife, you can have one with me.' When you treat the church right, *then* you can have a relationship. How am I going to have a relationship with God and treat my wife like dirt (*come on, now!*) (*can't do it.*)? And if the wife wants to have a relationship with God . . . she got to honor her husband. Oh, everybody so holy (*mm-hmm*) (*yeah, yeah, yeah*), but don't nobody want to treat nobody right (*come on, now!*). Yeah, you hold in *here* . . . but what about when you leave (*yesssir!*) the church arena? Huh? That's what God lookin' at. That *real* character, that *reeeeaal* character. It don't mean nothin' *in here*. When I ain't got Mother Brass's eyes on me, when Mother William ain't lookin' at me, can I still live holy? Can I still walk right? Can I still do . . . the right . . . thing (*fess up!*)? Folks need help. But folks don't come up that don't wanna come up, that ain't *ready* to come up. Folks ain't gave up the world yet. They ain't *gave up the world*. But you got to give up the world.

"Y'all not leave out this door today with your life messed up (*amen*). I don't care who you are, if you in this building today, you came here 'cause you sick.

"I got a prescription (*ha!*). I *haaave* a prescription (*yeah, yeah, yeah*). And you ain't got to pay for it. It's free. God got some anti-biotics, and some penicillin. If you *want* it, you can get it. And be healed, yessir."

Cook bid us stand. "God can change us," he said. "I don't care who you are, I don't care where you are. If you want Jesus to change you, He can do it. Oh, yes, He can do it. But you got to want it.

"Now, see, one thing about you, when you hear the Word and the Word find you, don't no call had to be made. You should start coming out. Because that's when you should be about the Word of God. But when you *really* ready to get serious about your walk with God, after the message, you ought to start *running* to Him, and ask God to help you (*amen*). Is there anybody here that need prayer?" From the pews across the aisle, women rustled and moved toward the center—clapping, but not over-joyed, with a serious, focused passion. The women drifted in clusters toward Pastor Cook—a line, finally, but only after they'd walked forward a little. They walked toward his touch and private speech, the microphone pressed against his mouth, with the elder and younger lieutenants flanking him and hold-ing the soul who'd braved the few steps up to submit to Cook's rhythmic power, to confess, channel, and be healed. The women swayed and chattered; the women clapped. There was a surge building underneath this incantation, a dolorous joy. The hus-band in front of me had slipped out of the pew earlier, and I'd missed where to, but then the sound of drums rattling from behind the pulpit caught up to us, sneaking in underneath the voices. I looked over and could see the husband now, seated, with a bass in his lap, nodding at the drummer. The drums began to tick and rattle and thump. The bass awakened, very slowly. The music built an awkward thunder, a slow riff with thick slow jukes and fills woven in the hook, underneath the moody ecstasy of the congregation. The hook fed the chaos just enough, and Pastor Cook held the mic close to his mouth, and he was pouring out a litany, his voice tearing the woofer: "*ohh-pen* yourmouth, *ohh-pen* yourmouth, *ohh-pen* yourmouth—*thank*Him*thank*Him*thank* Him. And while you're thanking Him, *receeeive* Him." A storm of sorts, a thing with its own cataclysmic happiness. The toddler boy in front of me seemed irritated, and began to wail. It *was* frightening . . . but seductive. "Don't stop thanking Him," Cook said. "Keep thanking Him. Hands up, everybody."

And the women began to lose themselves as that bass line slid around the room. One woman spoke in tongues, in rapture, gushing forth—hallelujah, hallelujah, hallelujah ("*It's*allright *it's*allright *it's*allright *it's*allright," Cook hollered)—and she spilled a deep, low ululation out into the room. God or not, we were in the presence of something visceral and real. A girl—sixteen, big boned—began to shriek, and her arms whipped back against her face, jerking free of some shackle, popping, and she swung and slapped and spun out into the aisle, she couldn't stand it, and threw herself against the pew in front of us, as if unaware it was even there, and unaffected by the pain of slamming into that wood. She kept screaming in ecstasy. I began to tremble just a little. My neck began to sweat. A woman eased across to the aisle to hold her still. No one was startled, there was no emergency. This was the ritual: God was in the room. There was no cynicism or logic powerful enough to push back against this suffocating emotion—rather, it was resistance to this ecstasy that triggered a slight suffering in me, as if a pressure had swelled simply from trying to make sense of things. So I began to let go . . .

. . . but didn't . . .

I sat, and hunkered behind the mother and child in the pew in front of me. Tears welled up, but I wiped at them. It was as if I'd been dragged by a sound toward a door, and was allowed to hold it and choose, hand on the handle, whether to open it, knowing that another state of joy I recognized and feared waited on the other side. So I fell away, feeling a coward, but back in my right place, just shy of ecstasy. Deliverance, for now, would have to wait. And suddenly I felt as tired as if I'd crawled a mile.

The joy wound down, gradually. The women across the aisle began praying to themselves. Cook downshifted, addressing a brother or sister or mother of the congregation as to his or her particular issue that week. He brought up a few logistical matters, casually, as if we'd gathered here for lunch. "Let me ask y'all something—where Mother Carver? You all want to start coming out on Wednesday and Friday at six thirty? Mother Carver, she asked me about that. And I understand why, because it gets dark earlier, and it's kind of convenient. How does everybody feel about it?" He looked around. The congregation shrugged and muttered. Folks hesitated, but it wasn't too popular a move. Cook turned to her, apologetic. "I have to consider everybody," he said. "I know Minister Irving gets off his thing at six. I know he work those late hours. And when he *can* get here, it's a blessing, and I don't want to cut *that* out. Praise God. So, you know, this might be one we have to pass on, Mother. Got to pass on it. But if I have to escort you home, I will."

"Amen."

"All hearts and minds are clear?"

Then he saw me. "Oh, yessir, would you like to stand up and say something?"

The congregation turned and watched. I felt a fever in my neck.

"Do I need to?"

"No, sir. We just giving you a choice."

I blurted out: "I do appreciate you allowing me to visit and spend the service with you."

A few folks said, "Amen."

"What church you fit into?" Cook asked.

"I'm visiting from out of town."

"Out of town."

"I'm Catholic. I'm a friend of the deacon."

"Okay, all right, all right," said the elder.

"Well, we glad to have you, sir," Cook said.

And the congregation nodded hello, and folks smiled, and Logan smiled, too. I breathed and grinned a wide grin at him—relieved, almost joyful.

"All hearts and minds are clear?" asked the pastor. "Let us stand."

We stood, and Pastor Cook thanked God, and asked us to pray for Bernie's daughter, that she have a successful delivery, and we sang, and he blessed us, and we dispersed, with hands and hugs extended to me, with even the bassist father turning to hug and welcome me, and with encouragements to come again.

"We're doing great right now," Logan said. The church had emptied but for the three of us—Logan, myself, and his new wife. He seemed happy to see me, and eager to fill me in on his life since the spring. "We're renting in Brandon now," he said. Things were slowly falling into place for him. "We're trying to straighten up credit," he said, "because it messed up a lot of credit issues in my life before, and now we're trying together as one—just trying to *cope* with things."

He was working at a glass company, the same job he'd just gotten when we'd met. As for his wife, they had met here, when Logan's sister invited her to a revival in January. They'd married a month later. A month after that, we were trashing out his house.

"You know, I brought a lot of excess baggage into this marriage. And she was just . . . good. She was a God-fearing woman, and she accepted me and everything that went along with that. She came to the house. No lights on . . . fleas. You been there. And out of all of that, she *still* . . . but it was something . . . it wasn't in our control. God ordained us to be together. I really believe if it had not been, she would have looked at this and said, 'Man, I ain't gonna let myself get mixed up with that guy. He all messed up financially, he this and he that.' But because the God that's in her let her know about the God in me, that there was going to be a change."

"And I questioned God," she said. "Why He put me with someone that's like that. The home all messed up. His credit messed up. He got fleas everywhere. He living dirty. But God let me know that there's something better coming in the end, so . . ."

Logan spoke of God touching him, but I'd always wondered how anyone recognized that touch. The phone ringing, the mail piling up, the fleas, the utilities blinking off one by one, our notes on the door . . . how could he have distinguished between God's touch and the lesser answer?

"*Faith*," he said, unspooling the word and the word that followed, "*peace*. When you receive God in your life, it's a voice that tells you something. You hear people, like, 'How you know it wasn't the devil?' I knew it wasn't the devil because of that peace. There's peace and there's no confusion. It's a door that's already open. And the devil ain't ever gonna lead you in no right direction. He's never gonna do that 'cause his nature won't allow him to do that. The Bible says that all perfect gifts is from heaven. Now, He *allows* certain things to happen to us that ain't a perfect gift, but we know He is in control. But when you're saved, there's this voice. Sometimes we question that voice. But He'll let you know."

I wasn't sold, though I wanted to be. I *had* felt something here this morning, but I wasn't sure what I would call it, wasn't sure if I happened to be a sucker for a certain public-performance equation. I was brought to tears at a jazz show once, with just a couple of drinks in me, so I had to consider that I might be a sentimentalist.

They were renting, he said, and hoped they could buy the house at some point. The landlord had made a deal with them. So far, they were keeping up. "I don't look about my past no more," he said. "It's just what it is. Now, there's some things got to be answered in my past, but I don't worry about it no more. I learn from my mistakes. When I get another home, I can keep it. See, a lot of things that look bad ain't bad. I look at it in a positive way. I *learn* something out of it. It's like when I went to prison: I learned. It was a teacher to me. I could help someone else. You know, once you come into the light of things, it becomes knowledge. And knowledge is power."

Logan never asked about his old house on Hillsborough. I wouldn't have had much to tell him. I knew that it had gone to auction, and had been bought cheap—$26,000—but I didn't expect a metamorphosis when I drove by to see it.

By then I'd learned to cut through city shortcuts to get to Sulphur Springs, using the old water tower as a landmark. The neighborhood had changed a little since my last visit. Across the street, the yard where I'd met a trash-out couple was packed with cousins who'd arrived for a cookout. A Dominican family was renting the place. Kids shrieked and ran and rode their bikes up and down the street. A pair of pit bulls next door snarled at the ruckus. I looked over and saw two sullen-looking dudes on Pops's old stoop. They had no idea who Pops was, and didn't much care for my asking, either. George was still around, but he barely remembered me, and anyway the game was on.

The deacon's old house was now the brightest on the block, painted white with lime-green shutters, a lime-green door. Even the front patio, just a length of concrete that ran across the front of the house, and about the depth of a sidewalk, had been painted the same bright-lollipop green. I hadn't even noticed the patio the last time here; now it seemed like a perk. An iron railing had been added for decoration. Mulch lined the edge, with small palm fronds planted here and there. Most of the sand in the yard had been raked away, exposing a driveway, a U-shaped strip of concrete with a strip of healthy grass in the middle. A concrete-and-stone path snaked from the chain-link fence to the door. A cinder-block bench was perched in front of a tree, its limbs lopped off, the top shorn away as if blasted by lightning, less a tree than a tall, rashy totem. The bench under the tree must have been intended as a charming touch, but even in the sunlight they seemed like props for *Godot*.

A worker emerged from inside the house, talking in Spanish on a cell phone, looked at me, then sat on the bench. I could barely pick up on the conversation, some intense discussion of the price of tile. A woman dressed in jeans and with a clipboard came out next, relaying something to the worker so he could relay it over the phone. She was followed by a couple of guys—one tall and big-framed, very heavy, like a retired wrestler; the other white-haired and with a hangdog look. The big fellow's name was Joe, that's all he would share. His anonymity notwithstanding, he was chatty, shaking his large cup of soda and ice, sipping from it, filling me in.

The other fellow was Alan Frazier, and Alan kept his distance for a while, circling the conversation, glancing at us while he inspected the house. He and Joe had bought this house at the last REDC auction that rolled through town. They were investors and knew the block well: Joe's wife had tried to sell the house next door, without luck; they'd tried to buy the foreclosure across the street (they were outbid at $30,000) and the one on the corner (it went for $22,500). When Joe saw the deacon's house in the REDC catalog, he pulled the trigger. "Just based on the picture," he said.

"That's a hell of a crapshoot," I said.

He shrugged. "It's what I do," he said, and besides, buying blind included all kinds of surprises, not all of them disappointments: Mets memorabilia, shotguns, diamonds, etc.

How could anyone buy a house without seeing it first?

They both answered at once: "The price."

"The potential is in future values," Frazier said, meaning that money is made over time as the price of real estate improves—or, in this case, recovers. Frazier talked as if he were coming out of a slumber, more of a sleepy, nasal moaning than a slur, with an exhausted expression that matched his voice.

Had any blind buys turned out to be disasters?

Joe shook his cup. "What do you call a disaster?"

"Unsalvageable."

"No," he said. "It's *never* unsalvageable. You get *something*. The worst house I bought, nobody told me when I bought it that it was on a sinkhole. But it wasn't unsalvageable." In fact, he'd made a profit. He bought the house for $42,000, then sold it and agreed to finance the mortgage to a fellow for $125,000. Soon *that* buyer wanted out and, according to Joe, began digging through county records to find any loopholes that might help. "That's how he discovered the sinkhole," Joe said. "So he sued me and he showed everybody where he thought the sinkhole was, and looking at this crack on the floor we said, 'Yeah, this is a sinkhole.' Nobody knew! He had to go through the paperwork, rip up the carpet and the padding, and there it was. So I gave him a reduction in the mortgage." The buyer defaulted anyway, and Joe foreclosed. As luck would have it, the market was on an upswing. "I got to sell the house *and* disclose that it was on a sinkhole for eighty thousand. I got lucky. The guy I disclosed to didn't care."

Joe spoke with a wet speech. He sounded drunk, but he knew his trade, and had his math down cold. His swagger was impressive, and though real estate generally took guts, you didn't meet guys like Joe too often. He was among the more exclusive club of high-risk deed slingers. He gambled, but he was blasé about the risks and the amount of money he threw around. I saw his type at the courthouse, during foreclosure auctions as the clerk rattled off the case numbers and asking prices—a dull, almost mind-numbing ceremony in a time when no one but the banks wanted the properties. Those courthouse urchins—the investors, the legal processors, the would-be landlords—all carried themselves with an air of existential boredom, the antithesis of the hyperactive panic of the real estate agents. Joe was of that breed who had spent decades in the halls of county offices crunching numbers, clawing through files, and seemed to have mastered the deadening tedium of regulations and laws. His breeziness with money was either the result of his apparent wealth or the secret to it, or both. Not even the nightmare scenarios earned more than a shrug.

But Joe was careful to point out the difference between his nonchalance and corruption. "I know a few investors I would never deal with," he said. "They're dirty. Dirty as the floor. I know guys that record bogus deeds. They make up their own deeds and record it. If somebody says, 'Okay, I'm going to foreclose on you,' the first person that gets to write a claim is the one that's got the bogus deed in there." He shook his cup and kept talking, getting a kick out of my reaction to just how ruthless real estate could be. His line of work included the tax auction, an especially cruel way to make a living. "Basically, if a home-owner or condo owner owes property taxes long enough, the property gets auctioned off every Wednesday at the courthouse steps." Joe recounted how he had often gone down to the Wednesday auctions, paid the lien, which was just a fraction of what the property was worth, then showed up at the property with the deed in hand, asking if the now former owner would like to buy it back. "Then the lawyers get involved, and we figure it out," he said. He smiled. "But that's the lowest thing I do."

They let me snoop through the house to see the repairs they'd done. Inside, the walls were a bright white, a strong sun angling in through the curtainless windows, bright enough that you had to squint. The security grates seemed almost elegant. It took three coats of paint to get the walls that white, Joe said. Bright as it was, empty as it was, the house seemed twice as spacious as I remembered it. Lightbulbs were attached to the sockets. The floors were a black concrete base still, the tile on its way. The bathrooms had been scrubbed. It was the same kitchen we'd attacked back in spring, but seemed expanded by the air and light and paint. I hadn't even noticed that the bedroom ceilings were paneled in wood.

Frazier walked in and joined me.

I complimented the house.

"It's well built," he said, clearly admiring it. "Plaster wall, not drywall."

I pointed to a blinking alarm console attached to the living room wall. "This new?"

"That's fake."

"You think it's going to *scare* anybody?"

"Well, if they look in, they see the little blinking light."

All this work, in the end, would be to sell the house again for an asking price of $100,000. I balked at the price. "We found out people in the area are selling for *ninety*," Alan said, a little defensive but also not quite believing it, either. "But we'll give it to you for ten grand down. Just make the payments." They weren't too keen on financing it, since that meant less money in the short run, which meant less money to invest and less money to make. They preferred selling their houses outright. The last thing they wanted, they agreed, was to rent.

They'd have a hard time selling that house for a hundred thousand in Sulphur Springs. Still, Frazier spoke fondly of the neighborhood's history. "The streetcar from Tampa ended right there," he said, pointing east. "People would come for the winter for the sulphur waters, and they built all these little cottages around here for their winter homes, all these little houses that you see."

This was, back in the '20s, one of the more popular getaways in Tampa, when the developer Josiah Richardson built an amusement park that included an alligator farm, a shopping arcade, bath houses, a dance pavilion, and a toboggan slide that dumped riders into a pond. But the park's success didn't prevent Richardson from falling into bankruptcy, and eventually, just about everything he'd built was shuttered. His only legacy was a dilapidated water tower, seldom visited. The rest was razed to expand parking for the dog track.

Frazier leaned against the front door. His face had a green tint from the sunlight bouncing off the patio. Before leaving us, Joe shook his cup and teased him, relishing that he was divulging some ironic secret. "You know that Alan's an aristocrat," he said.

"A broke aristocrat," Frazier said, smiling wearily.

"He's a Hendry," Joe said, chuckling, and walked to his car.

By Hendry, Joe meant Hendry County, named for the Hendry clan of cattle barons who amassed great tracts of land after the Civil War, and whose cattle grazed what they could of the scrappy land south of Lake Okeechobee, feeding on the edges of the Everglades. At one time, the Hendrys were known as "the Cattle Kings of Florida," a bittersweet legacy for Frazier now.

He went to the sink and soaked some paper towels, wiped the counter, then filled a cup with water to take outside: The plants looked dry.

THE next time I saw Alan Frazier, later that winter, he'd been reconsidering the tenant option. Joe had sold his half of the house to Alan after losing tens of thousands of dollars mistiming Bank of America stock. In six months Frazier hadn't gotten a single call inquiring about the house. "It's a nice house," he said, "but it's hard to sell something in this neighborhood." He was hesitant to finance the mortgage, since the slower cash flow would hinder his ability to flip other properties.

"Why not rent to own?" I said. "You're not going to sell this."

"You don't think so?"

"No."

He gently kicked the grass and looked around.

"I might finance it," he said. "But I want ten thousand down."

I mentioned what the deacon had said, that he actually missed living here. And that he was anxious to own again. He was in a rent-to-own situation already.

"Does he have cash?"

I didn't know.

By then, the TARP's Neighborhood Stabilization Program had allocated $19 million to Hillsborough County. Frazier was hoping that the influx of cash would give him a chance to sell the house to the city. But the chances of that happening were slim, since most of the money was dedicated to getting housing assets off the banks' books. "If they just gave the money to the city and said, 'Go buy as much as you can,' they could do a lot more. And it would help a lot more poor people. But that's not the goal. The goal is to stabilize prices and help the banks, not to help the poor." His only choice, really, was to sit and wait. "I'm going to advertise it and try to get somebody to buy it—you know, tell them I'll pay closing costs, everything. If they have *any* chance of getting a mortgage, I'll subsidize it. Anything to help them get it. It's a nice house." He glanced around. "The problem is the neighborhood."

He kept vacillating. "I don't know. Maybe I'll hold on until things turn a little. I own it free and clear. Taxes are a couple thousand a year. But I owe twenty-five in back taxes, I gotta sell *something*. I got a lot of properties. But nobody can get financing, everything is shut down right now."

A kid on an enormous tricycle rode slowly past us, with a living-room speaker strapped by a bungee cord to the back, between the rear wheels. He blasted a slow, thumping love song, loud enough that we had to shout, and even then not quite able to hear each other. The kid weaved, creeping along, as if to dare anyone on the block to holler at him. Or maybe it was a Sunday tradition, like the ice-cream man, this kid weaving along, block by block, putting people in the mood on a Sunday afternoon with this apocalyptically loud fuck jam.

Another inspection: an L-shaped ranch made of red-and-white brick, with a wide, cracked driveway and a cluster of citrus trees in the back. This house sat across from what was technically a city park but was really just a low retention pond, its banks choked with overgrowth. Ugly as the pond was, the rest of the block was well kept, sun-dappled, pleasant. You could hear children chirping in the schoolyard a block away.

Our routine unfolded: the ticking engine, jets scraping across the sky, the buzz of saws and the gurgle of single-props delivering afternoon traffic reports. We walked up the cracked driveway, opened the storm door, knocked, and waited. Junk mail was scattered on a table out front, and by the name printed on it we knew the owner was Hispanic. I peeked through the window, looking in between the open blinds, and saw enough furniture where it seemed to belong, not shifted out of place, no signs of any hectic moves. "People still live here," I muttered.

I walked around the east side of the house, through an enormous lot of dry grass tall as my waist, shaded here and there by a handful of cankered orange trees. Burrs covered my jeans within just a few steps, and it didn't take too many more steps for me to turn around and give up. I could see a pool's green water through the loose pickets of a short wood fence, as if to keep a child from falling in.

Dad began writing the note, with Mena's card taped to it: *Por favor llamen a Mena Reyes lo mas pronto posible.*

"Tell them why," I suggested.

He called Mena to double-check if he could write anything more specific, and shortly hung up. "No cash for keys yet," he said. But he added a line: *Ella trabaja con el banco.*

I spotted a neighbor weeding her garden, and jogged over to ask if she'd seen anyone come and go from this place, any signs of life. All she could tell me was that there had been a FOR SALE sign out front, which was gone now. I mentioned the sign to Dad, who flipped through the paperwork. "Yeah, it was listed at $289,000," he said.

"For this sucker?"

"And they probably paid more than that."

Again, as in so many cases, the price and the home failed to connect. The house was charming, sure, but it was worth maybe half the debt on paper.

"The trick here will be to come at night," Dad said. "To see if the lights are on."

Which we never got around to doing, though I did, after leaving my card on the door, and writing my own notes, and driving past the house now and then, finally meet its owner. It was a Saturday morning. The garage was open, with furniture and books and toys and appliances spilling out and across the driveway, all for sale. About a dozen different mirrors flashed in the sun. A tiny pleather recliner, fifty bucks; a squirt shotgun, five bucks. A potted palm didn't have a tag.

Deep in the shade of the garage, a middle-aged man sat watching Univisión, the volume cranked up, Christmas commercials in full stride. The owner, I guessed, was the fellow slouched on the cast-iron bench by the front door. His name was Carlos. He was chubby in his orange-and-blue undershirt, his arms stretched across the back of the bench. His face was a little hidden in a cap set low and thick glasses.

I told him who I was, and mentioned the notes I'd left, and he nodded but didn't show much interest. I explained that I was writing about foreclosures, and wondered if he'd mind talking a bit about what he'd been going through.

"I'm kind of busy," he said softly, nodding toward the junk for sale. With his lilt, his refusal didn't sound so convincing. I turned and looked at the driveway. I was, technically, his only customer. So I shuffled over to the tables and began browsing, scanning the books, testing a fishing reel, and asked him what he did for a living.

He was a truck driver, he said, mostly local routes—supermarkets and such. He'd lived in Florida for about fifteen years, having moved from up North, and he lost his job several months ago after he and his wife split up. She took their five-year-old girl with her. After his wife left—even when she was around, but certainly once she'd left—the payments on this house, which they'd refinanced over and over again, began to overwhelm him.

I asked if he had tried to call Mena, which I knew he hadn't. He shrugged.

"You should," I said. There was a good possibility that if he called her, and was convincing, she might be able to convince the bank to give him money to move. I couldn't promise anything, and was taking a risk just by suggesting this was an option. I hadn't talked to Mena about it. His departure from this house was inevitable, we both knew that much. "Do you know where you're going to go?"

He shook his head and smirked. "Not yet," he said.

"Anybody you can stay with?"

He just barely shook his head again. He'd been spending his days looking for work, he said—"looking in the paper, you know, just go around to big companies and stuff. But a lot of places are telling me that they're firing, so it hasn't been that easy. I can probably get a job, but I'll have to go long distance, out of state. But I don't want to travel, especially not north, where it's getting cold and it's snowing, and the mountains . . ."

He meant trucking, of course, but why stick with it? Why not look for something else?

"I don't have anything else that I can do," he said. "I'm skilled in some other things, but if you don't have any background on it, nobody's going to hire you and stuff, you know? I been working in trucking for a long time and if I go to an electrician place, they're not looking for no truckers. Even if I could do it and stuff, you know? That's the problem."

I asked him how his divorce affected the foreclosure. He chuckled. "When you have two people working in a house and stuff, and you make a certain amount of money . . . sometimes, you know, it's good. But when one person loses their job—or both of them, you know?—or you find a job and it's not going to pay the same thing as you was making before—and a lot of people, these mortgages and stuff, they got screwed up. After two or three years pass by, you know, they have adjustables, so the interest goes up and, you know, three or four hundred dollars that it goes up and stuff, you know? It's hard. We refinanced and stuff, but the mortgage that we had was for three years, right? And we spent, like, thirteen hundred and something dollars a month, and after the three years it shot up. It went to fifteen or sixteen hundred dollars and stuff.

"I didn't know it was going to happen when they first give me the mortgage and stuff. There's people, most people in mortgages, they crooked and stuff. They just want to get the business. They don't even try to disclose to you the interest and all of that stuff, you know? They just want your business and get out."

However reticent he may have been initially, he was on a roll now, in a monologue of injustice and financial straits. There was something childlike in his verbal tics, the way he glanced at his shoes and kicked the dust, hands in pockets, shifting his weight until he worked his way through a convoluted explanation of the chicanery of mortgage brokers, and could finally drive home the point he'd originally wanted to make. I was inclined to believe that he'd been taken advantage of, but because he couldn't articulate exactly what had happened—as if, despite being in the thick of it, the problem nonetheless had to be explained to him, and memorized, and stored in separate parts of his mind he stretched to connect; as if he understood that solace was promised if he could follow a script in which the incomprehensible enemy was called out—and because he couldn't even remember the name of the company that had sold him the mortgage in the first place, that was responsible for this injustice that had been done to him, I started to get a sick feeling of doubting him. He couldn't remember the full name of the broker who had sold them their mortgage. He could only say that the guy was some vague "friend" named Michael. "Those people went out of business already," he said. "I guess you know why. Most mortgage companies are all like that. They all crooked, bro."

A small, elderly man in shorts walked up and inspected a record player (two bucks) and kept browsing.

The last payment Carlos made, he said, was over a year ago. "I been living here for about a year without paying a damn thing and stuff," he said. "It's a shame these banks don't work with you. I know they sold the house to a bank, a mortgage company for cheap. I don't even want to say what they sold it for, but they should've worked out something with me. They wanted fifty thousand. Who the hell has fifty thousand?"

"You haven't saved?"

"I haven't been working! I was collecting—about three hundred a week—but that don't even pay the food you eat. How am I going to save? I recently started with a job. I worked for a month, but it didn't work out. What money can I save?"

He kept trying to remember the name of the mortgage company, walking me through the loan. "We bought the house for $80,000. We refinanced it a number of times and we got up to $170,000 and, you know, with all the backup taxes and payments, we were at $220,000."

Why did he keep refinancing? "We did want to buy some things and, as times got harder, try to fix the house or to do something. You learn, you know. I never do that again, refinance a house. Anybody who refinances a house to get money out, you gotta be nuts to do that. Why you gonna take out thirty thousand, pay it off in thirty years, and blow it on nothing? It's going to cost you two hundred thousand for that money, you understand? If anybody asks me, don't get credit cards, don't refinance your house to buy something, because it's not worth it."

A wind was picking up.

"How long do you plan to stay?"

"I thought I had till the end of the month," he said. "The bank's been contacting me, but I'm not answering the phone. Somebody passed by, but I never saw them—the lady from the real estate."

This lady was Mena, of course, who he knew from the notes my father and I had taped to his door. I wasn't quite sure what the rules were, what the law was, whether I could make an offer that didn't already exist, but I did explain the *possibility* of working out a cash-for-keys deal. He should at least call her. "I would talk to her," I insisted. "I don't know how much it will be, but it helps."

"I'm here until they come and throw me out, to tell you the truth. Because I have nowhere to go, you know. I don't answer my phone to nobody, to tell you the truth. 'Cause I got creditors trying to hit me, and I just don't pick up. What am I going to tell them, you know? 'Hey, I haven't found a job!' You know?"

His brother, in the garage. "What about staying with him?" But he was one of three living together in a trailer. Not an option. I was stumped—but feeling foolish, too, because I wasn't in the business of lighting a fire under this guy's ass. The guilt of the work, both in knowing I'd come here on eviction day, and prying now to extract his story, was leading to some foolish overtures. Where else had he been looking for work?

"The paper. I'll pick up the Sunday paper to see if there's anything in there. I usually look to the supermarket at those employment magazines and stuff."

I suggested construction.

"I don't know if I want to do that. I'm not into it. I don't like it and stuff. And I don't know too much construction, to tell you the truth. And to start some kind of training right now, with my bad credit—most schools they check your credit, for financing and stuff."

He countered every suggestion with a reason not to pursue it. I looked around for something to buy.

"If that lady calls again," I said, "I encourage you to talk to her. At this point, it can only help. I have no idea when the bank is going to send—"

"Like I said before," he said, "I stay here until they come and throw my ass out, 'cause what am I gonna do? If I was to get a job . . . maybe. But to rent something you gotta have at least a job, and with my bad credit—any apartment house, they look at your credit."

Could his ex-wife help? It may have been a rude question, but I was getting desperate.

"She's in a situation, too," he said. "She gotta pay rent, so how can she help me? I haven't given her anything for the baby neither and stuff, you know?"

And with that detail, I'd crossed into a privacy I knew was off-limits. I looked at him, and he simply stood there reflecting a strength I lacked, as if his own ignorance and misfortune had endowed him with a cold wisdom, almost an arrogance, a steely indifference toward his eviction that made my confusion and frustration and questions—and strategizing *on his behalf*—look pitiful. I felt pathetic, and ignorant, and childish. He, on the other hand, seemed to have crossed into another state, beatified, slightly, by his gentle abandon.

That night, at dinner, things got a little tense at the table. I saw in Carlos an aspect of the problem that I hadn't yet encountered with anyone else. He was the first person I'd met who lacked the vigor that others, despite their terrible circumstances, had shown.

I expected he would end up in a shelter, or on the streets. And to have participated in any aspect of his ejection into that life was nauseating. The man needed help. I wanted to help him. "This guy is at the end of his rope," I told Mena. "I promise you that. I'm telling you, you need to pull out all the stops with this guy. He's *un poco bobito*, and maybe he's not trying hard enough, but he's somebody that got hit by one piece of bad luck after another, and he just doesn't feel like trying anymore."

I'm not sure what, exactly, I expected her to do. I at least wanted to get across to her that these might be extraordinary circumstances. I think she did understand this—or, at least, she seemed to recognize a victimization among some that was different from the recklessness of others. She, like Koebel, saw a lot of damning paperwork reflecting patterns of extravagance. And to accuse her of a failure to comprehend the foreclosure victim's circumstances was dangerous territory, because it drew upon the conflicting values we each possessed. She operated on the principle of accountability and fiscal responsibility, that if you don't pay your debts, you answer for it. This was my father's philosophy, the philosophy of people who had arrived in this country and worked themselves ragged. This was the philosophy of people who never refinanced. Carlos, on the other hand, had done so almost chronically.

So Mena was reluctant to ask the bank to extend a cash-for-keys offer, knowing Carlos wasn't interested. But I pressed her, and she agreed. She worried she might look foolish if he turned that thousand dollars down, but it was a foolishness worth risking.

———

A couple of days later, I found Carlos on his bench, tweaking the dial on his small radio to catch an AM station. He told me he'd spent the morning putting in a couple of job applications, then packing. The sun was on him at a hard angle, painting a burning gold on his face. He had to squint to see me.

"How'd the garage sale go?"

"Neither good or bad."

"What'd you end up selling?"

"*Porquería . . . chinchería*. Nothing big, man."

We were quiet a minute.

I explained that I'd talked to Mena, and told him she was going to try and get the bank to give him some cash to help move. He nodded. I explained the condition for the money, too, that he had to empty the place out himself. "We don't know what the bank is going to say, but could you use it?"

"How much are you talking about?"

"Five hundred dollars."

"Five hundred dollars, bro, that's not even enough to rent a place." He thought about it. "You know, for me to get out of here right now, five hundred dollars isn't going to kick it. I might as well stay here until they throw me out, 'cause I don't have no place to go, anyway. Five hundred isn't even going to help you move, to tell you the truth."

"I know it's not a lot. But it's *something*."

"It's something, but . . . it's nothing, man."

"Well, how much would you need?"

"I have no idea, bro."

He sat there, quiet. The radio blared commercials for joint pain, for dating Web sites, for Christmas shopping. A jet scraped low, a seashell roar. A woman announced a cure for cold sores.

I was stumped. He'd refused the money. And now what?

I started rambling. "Look, the bank is not going to overextend themselves. They are who they are. All I can say is, if you come up with a number, and call Mena back, and say, 'Look, you give me a thousand dollars—or fifteen hundred dollars, I don't know—I'll get all this stuff out of here.' And maybe it'll cost you two hundred to get rid of it all. And you've got around seven-fifty, that'll help you put a roof over your head, or *something*. You know what I mean? I'm just—I guess I . . . I don't even know why . . . I'm not supposed to get this involved. . . ."

He began to chuckle. "I hear you, man," he said, but I just kept talking.

And as I stuttered through his options, I noticed it: This chubby, lazy motherfucker was *laughing* at me—at my stammering, at my shyness, at my lack of composure. And as I talked I could feel his condescension, his strange confidence. And I kept talking, staring at a stuffed lizard he'd failed to sell, tossed onto a dresser he'd failed to sell.

This is why your wife left you, I thought.

I kept clicking my pen. "All I can say is that the only way to *get that money* (each word tapped on the notebook) is for you to call. If you don't call, they're going to assume that you don't care, and I know that's not true. I know that you're just pissed off and you're, you know, you're just *frustrated*. But if you call them, it won't hurt. It won't hurt to call. You know?"

Another plane flew low. There were only twenty minutes left in the trading day, the talk show host said. Apparently it had been a brutal day on Wall Street.

"Besides," it occurred to me, "this house might actually benefit from the Christmas moratorium. That might buy you time to find work."

"That's what I'm hoping for, bro!" he said, and chuckled again at the irony of it.

"It's my instinct not to trust a bank," I told him. "But you don't lose anything by calling them and telling them your situation. Say, 'All right, what if you give me two thousand.' And they might come back and say, 'No, we'll give you a thousand.' Shit, that's a thousand dollars!"

He nodded, then got up and turned off the radio. In the silence, the squeals of children reached us from the schoolyard across the field.

"Any luck looking for work?"

"I put in some more applications," he said. "Takes some time . . . you know . . . to get a response."

The birds chirped. The tiny voices refracted off the brick, and somehow doubled between buildings.

I looked toward the sun. "It's kind of nice out here."

"It's a beautiful day, yeah. It turned out nice."

"All right, well . . ." I looked at his neighbor's yard. "Is that grapefruit?"

"Yeah, the neighbor's tree."

"That must be nice."

An awkward silence. We both took a breath, and then I stepped over to shake his hand where he sat. Same promise: I'd let him know if anything else came to mind. He was grateful, and slouching there, seemed to say through the language of his repose, *Good luck, sucker.*

C arlos's eviction arrived on a cloudless, lazy January morning. Hector, Ismael, and I pulled up and parked on the
shoulder across the street. The sheriff's deputy wasn't due to
arrive for a short while. I could see carpet that had been ripped
out and rolled up and set on the side of the house. A garbage can
leaned on it. A dresser sat with its drawers cocked loose, like bad
teeth. I could see the bench Carlos had sat on the last time I was
here, smashed flat now in the grass. Cardboard boxes leaned
soaked and warped from the weather, outside for weeks.

We got out. Ismael limped gently down the street, stretching
and stepping like a fragile cat, staring up at the trees. Hector
leaned in through the driver's window. I leaned in through the
other. Our small talk was grumbling. The TARP had affected no
real changes on the ground that we could sense. Hector could
barely afford his house payments, and I could barely afford my
own. I mentioned the Byzantine nightmare of trying to modify
my mortgage, the paperwork, the waiting, the dead ends; he
mentioned the challenge of keeping up with his church's tithe.

A tithe seemed a bit unreasonable, considering the economic climate. But it paid dividends in its own way. "Do you think that I—working two, three, four days at most—could afford to pay a nine-hundred-dollar mortgage without His help?"

"So how do you do it?"

"God opens doors. It's like He says: 'Test me, try me, and I'll open the door to heaven. I will bless you. Bring me any challenge you've got. I challenge you: Bring me your tithe and I will bless you. It's like the Lord says: When you make an offering, do it happily, no regrets. Because God blesses that which pains you to do, but which you do happily. If you're going to give money to the church, do it happily, don't say, 'But I *need* that ten dollars, how can I give my last ten bucks?' So don't give it! And that's that. Don't give what you can't spare. But if you have faith in God, that He will bless you, He'll do it."

As he spoke, I could hear his pastor speaking, and imagined the artful hustle of this man "challenging" his flock to give 10 percent of what they had, and pocketing it.

"Listen," Hector said. "One time, a long time ago, I had six hundred in cash in my wallet—I'd counted it with my own hands, I'd touched it—and I needed seven hundred to pay the rent. I told God, 'I'm a hundred dollars short.' He heard me. He said, 'Go ahead, look! Count it!' So I looked—I counted it *twice*—seven hundred dollars."

"A miracle!"

"But it's *true*," he said, as if he anticipated my skepticism. "I've got no reason to lie to you, why should I? I can joke and bullshit with you and all that, but we're talking about something serious here. We'll all be tested. Just because I'm Christian doesn't mean I won't be tested. But we could suffer the same problems, be tested the same way. But there's a difference, and I'm going to tell you what it is: Your child could die, your brother or sister, or whatever else, but, in the middle of such tempests, you will find yourself in despair, but not me. Why? Because I possess a peace in my heart that you don't have. Only God can grant you that peace."

Should I have seen this story of Job coming? Perhaps, but Hector was well into it before I could stop him. He rallied through a long-winded improvisation, in which Job endured to became "the richest man in the village," with a youthful skin, to boot. "That's why you must stay faithful until you die. Because what are you going to take with you, from this world? Nothing. God loves souls. He hates to lose a single one. Believe it now or believe it when you're dead. Now you have an opportunity to redeem yourself. Once you've reached the afterlife, it's too late. Hold on a minute." He reached into his wallet and dug around a second. He handed me his pastor's card.

He was talking as the deputy turned the corner. She pulled up into the driveway. Ismael walked past and tapped the truck lightly as if to say, let's go.

The deputy had done fourteen evictions the day before, she said, and would try and knock out another eight today. She sounded Southern. She had a politely brusque way of speaking, singing gentle commands, but with just enough force that betrayed a meanness underneath the music. "We got a key? Lock? What we gotta do?" She was all hoof-and-whip. She walked straight up to the door, knocked—"sounds hollow" (she sang it)—announced herself (sang that, too, tough lilt, like calling the kids to dinner), "*Sher*-iff's *of*-fice," and waited to the count of *one*: "Drill! Let's go!"

Hector fumbled, trotted over with the screwdriver, and the deputy suffered very little of that. She walked over to the garage, twisted the handle. "This is open," she said, and waited for me to raise it, then walked in and sang her brisk "Sheriff's office!" call all through the garage and on into the house. "Gotta figure out where this house goes," she said. "Buncha rooms, isn't it!" She checked the closets, the bathrooms, shot outside to the workshed. Then her cell phone rang and she drifted away, chatting, returning once the call was over to get the paperwork out of the way.

And gone.

I began taking snapshots with the plastic camera: peanuts, a soda bottle, deodorant, cut-off jeans, a yardstick from Famous Tate Appliance and Bedding Center, pens, battered VHS tapes, cigar boxes—Carlos loved his cheap cigars. In his workshed, cans of WD-40, cans of bumper chrome spray, Fix-a-Flat, Desenex, Rust Not, Nu Finish, Bravo.

A plastic horse . . . five fire extinguishers, in different corners of the house, all upright.

The pool out back, hidden past the tall grass and the small privacy fence was telltale green, though nothing swam around in there. The grass was so tall, it drooped.

Finally, my father showed up, and began taking his own pictures. When I caught up to him by the front doorway—standing inside as I approached from the driveway—he *humphed*, staring at the wall. I leaned in and turned to see: taped to the wall were all the notes he'd left—*Por favor llamen a Mena. Ella trabaja con el banco*—as put there to trigger some internal debate each time Carlos stepped outside: Should I call?

Dad walked around. He marveled at the thoroughness with which the kitchen had been gutted. Practically the entire room was missing: cabinets, stove, fridge, sink, nothing but the plumbing fixtures sticking out, bare and useless, and only the glossy-pine railing that separated this room from the next was left.

Back outside, we watched a truck drive past, loaded to the hilt with fold-out chairs, a walker, a bedframe, crutches, washer dryer—all of it strapped down with a rope. I looked at him. "Metal pickers?"

"Yeah, go get 'em."

I chased and whistled after them and saw their taillights flicker at the end of the block as they turned and disappeared. Shortly we saw them as they came back around, pulling into the driveway, as close as they could get to all that scattered crap.

The driver got out, laughing with disbelief. "Somebody must've had rabies in this place!" Cuban, judging by his accent, the consonants nearly rubbed out.

We chuckled, but clarified. "The bank took it," Dad said.

He smiled and shook his head. *"No es fácil."*

"You guys work in construction?"

"I'm a mechanic," the driver said. "I got a shop down on South Street. But right now, really, the way things are—*floja, floja, floja.*"

"Got a card?" He didn't have one, but he gave us his number. Dad could always use a good metal man. He'd seen three or four come and go, and it was always better to put the tonnage to better use than the dump.

The driver was from Pinar del Río, he said. They chatted a bit about it, about where they were from, and joked about how fucked it was. He had a kid with him, not quite twenty, dark and quiet, and already picking through the metal. He too was from Pinar del Río, he said, shyly. He arrived about a year ago.

Was it difficult coming over?

"We took a boat," he said.

I imagined something small. "Was it dangerous?"

"A speedboat," he said, not looking at me, and I understood then what his shyness meant.

OPPORTUNITY
KNOCKS

Looking back, I have no excuses, other than naïveté, to explain why the equation between foreclosures and homelessness wasn't more obvious to me earlier. In all the years of cleaning up, reading a room, or standing idle while a deputy knocked and hollered and went through the motions of his cruel duty, I never imagined that the owners I'd met or erased from a place were enduring anything worse than the depressing inconvenience of living on a mother's couch or sleeping on a cousin's floor. I never connected their departure to the tent cities that began to spring up under bridges, or the parking lots that became villages for people living out of cars. It was easy to assume that whoever disappeared from a four-bedroom cookie cutter with a pool, however green and overrun with bugs or lizards, had at least one resource left, some emergency plan or phone call they could make on their way out before the sheriff's deputy showed up.

I do not know what happened to Carlos. He's never answered the cell phone number I have for him. But whatever happened to him, it was obvious that by the time we met, his resilience was spent. He seemed in danger, not of any kind of violence to himself, but of simply disappearing into a life on the street. This resonated, with strange timing. I became obsessed with the connection between foreclosures and homelessness, and in looking for it, discovered one of the most honest revolutionaries this crisis would produce.

———

For a while, for a season, there was a sense that a dramatic, galvanized response would form in proportion to the financial crisis itself. The holiday moratorium was lifted, and the recession triggered by the housing market collapse began to work a chokehold across the classes, the pain worsening as it descended toward the poor. And as the purge of homeowners accelerated, a resistance ramped up, driven by anger over the TARP bailout and a fresh story in which the nexus between foreclosures and homelessness began to widen, the emergency of homelessness inching its way up the social ladder, just a little.

The resistance evolved, from private acts of subterfuge across the country—setting traps of boiling water to burn whoever came to claim a house, or spreading ferret piles across the floor, or just hiding in the attic until the cleanup crew left—to more public acts of civil disobedience. In Philadelphia, in the spring of 2008, a March meeting of the city council ended with a unanimous resolution that called for a moratorium on foreclosures. It was unenforceable, initially, but became a catalyst when the Philadelphia County Sheriff, John Green, backed it up, canceling the next day's foreclosure auction. Sheriff Green's move wasn't exactly legal, but that technicality got lost in the popular response to his move. It took about a day or so for him to become a national personification of resistance—a government employee, no less—armed with his own "Declaration of Neighborhood Stability" and "Sheriff Green's Important Steps to Saving Your Home." What's more, his standoff got results: Just a few days after the moratorium, a pair of circuit court judges huddled with lenders' lawyers and housing advocates to broker a compromise, a pilot program that included "conciliation conferences" between lenders and homeowners to help keep people in their homes. It served as a model, but was seldom applied in other courts and other states.

Then there was Sheriff Thomas Dart, of Chicago, frustrated by the number of "completely stunned" tenants he and his deputies were kicking out onto the streets, who finally refused to carry out any evictions until the circuit court implemented steps to warn tenants of a landlord's impending foreclosure (the measure took about a week, no time to waste). Dart ended up sharing the grisly details of his job at a hearing before the Senate Judiciary Committee in November, where he testified alongside David G. Kittle, chairman of the Mortgage Bankers Association, as part of a hearing on a bill that would give judges the power to adjust home mortgages in bankruptcy. Kittle and Dart were a blunt pairing, but it set the poles. Dart described his many visits to Chicago's Englewood neighborhood, where, during a spate of foreclosures, sixteen homes were reduced to four after demolition, and two of the remaining four were boarded up. "It's absolute chaos out there," Dart told the committee. Kittle took a more distant, philosophical position, reminding the committee that, as part of the natural free-market cycle, "some people have to fail."

Committees, state agencies, hotlines, Hope Now, foreclosure-defense lawyers (a hot new market): The institutional responses

were ad hoc and arthritic. But there were a handful of real revolutionaries, frustrated by the pomp and circumstance of con-
gressional hearings and the false charity of lawyers. Bruce Marks
was one of them, an outspoken hybrid between activist mortgage broker and radical provocateur. Marks made a name for
himself and his organization, the Neighborhood Assistance
Corporation of America, by terrorizing bank CEOs—dumping
furniture on their lawn, bull-horning them on Saturday mornings, publishing, on his Web site, their pictures and phone numbers and whatever dirty laundry he could find. He harassed
them into cooperation, and got some results, with a handful
of major lenders—Bank of America and Wells Fargo among
them—agreeing to work with homeowners in trouble.

Ohio Congresswoman Marcy Kaptur was another, remarkable for the fact that she, like Sheriffs Green and Dart, was an
elected official using civil disobedience on behalf of her constituency. She became a citizen's hero in January 2009 when she
spoke on the House floor and advised homeowners to stand firm
against foreclosure, to stay put and squat their own foreclosed
homes until the lender produced the note that proved its rightful
ownership, an act that was especially difficult since so many
mortgages had been tranched tenfold and the paperwork lost.
Ultimately, Kaptor's advice only went so far; there was little to
nothing a homeowner could actually do once the bank did
finally produce the note, foreclose on the house, and send the
sheriff's deputy to evict them. But it did arm people with enough
confidence to fight and buy a little time, and it did generate
enough attention to force banks and servicers to practice better
diligence.

Then there was Max Rameau, a Miami activist whose guer-
rilla mission was a radical blend of solutions, summed up in an

Associated Press article in December 2008: "He is helping home-less people illegally move into foreclosed homes." Rameau called it "liberating" a home.

It was an irresistible story, and very simple: Rameau and his organization, Take Back the Land, contended that everyone, no matter what—the new and old faces of homelessness alike—deserved a home. He also considered the surplus of empty, dete-riorating foreclosures a gross waste of a precious resource. The misdemeanor of trespassing didn't dissuade him; trespassing was the point. Rameau wanted the real estate agent, the bank, the cops all to know. And should they decide to try and kick a family out, he wanted that confrontation to be broadcast to the public, hoping to provoke a very public debate over what land rights were in the first place.

I tracked him down, studied what stories I could find on him. I brought my father to hear him speak in Sarasota, at a small, private college—a surreal scene, given the wealth and leisure that distinguished this coastal town. And I began to get to know him. In all our conversations, he stressed that Take Back the Land was not a homeless-advocacy group. "We are not a home-less organization," he said emphatically. "We are not a *housing* organization. Our issue is land and land control." Specifically, the black community's right to control land in the black com-munity. Homelessness, then, was the issue through which he could address his larger concerns, and foreclosures, in turn, were the occasion for taking a closer look at homelessness. This had been his mission for some time, but it was now, in the throes of the crisis, that the mission dovetailed neatly with an agitated public. It was as if foreclosures were the crisis Rameau had been waiting for all this time. And he wasn't shy about his mission. He was, in fact, looking for a fight.

I met up with Rameau in February at his office in Miami, tucked in an anonymous storefront on the corner of Sixty-eighth Street and Fifteenth Avenue, in the heart of Liberty City. The day I showed up, the avenue was empty, hardly any cars or people, wide and flanked by dead-still merchants and rickety homes. The bodega across the street showed a mural of Cuban sandwiches and hot dogs, beer and Pepsi, and Martin Luther King, Jr. A driveway led to a patio, through which I saw a couple of dudes enter and exit the bodega. A PA system was crammed in there somewhere; Lil' Wayne's "Mrs. Officer" throbbed between the buildings. The song was on a loop; when it ended, it started right back up again.

Inside the office, I found Max in a small cubicle, slouched as far back as his swiveling chair would allow. He was updating Take Back the Land's Facebook page. He stood up, greeted me. He was smaller than I expected, medium height, and slightly pudgy. He had a soft, boyish face, the sad eyes of a crooner. The cubicle was packed tight: a pile of computer monitors stacked in one corner, computer shells stacked in another, a trio of recycling cans, and a set of house speakers tucked inside a homemade cabinet that rested above his desk. Next to the stack of monitors, on a side table, were about a dozen coconuts in a pile, a gift for his yard.

I snooped around the office while he finished up. The space was simple, a long, narrow room painted pale yellow. On one wall was a GoogleMaps collage of the neighborhood, with a color code that helped distinguish the rooftops—green meant foreclosed, yellow meant a church, red meant vacant, and orange meant a government building. Across from that, a hodgepodge of donated titles filled a bookshelf: *A Time for Peace* by Mikhael Gorbachev, *eBay for Dummies, mp3 for Dummies, Domain Names for Dummies, Creating Web Pages for Dummies*, a book on American civics, a book on China, *The Sixties Papers, Great Jews in Sports* . . .

Toward the back, the place looked more like an electronics repair shop, with more monitors and cases, most of them dismantled. Rameau's plan was to replace the motherboards and install the Linux operating system ("It's free," he explained, "it's cheap, and I myself am very partial to open source."). He was also hoping to get a T-1 line set up by the weekend, and to have a wireless tower installed on the roof. Once all the equipment was in place, and the wireless cards were installed, he could then sell the computers for twenty-five bucks a pop to anyone living in the neighborhood, fifty bucks if they lived outside it, so that people living outside the neighborhood could help subsidize the progress of those inside—thinking locally, acting locally.

Of the seven families Take Back the Land had moved into empty houses back in the fall of 2007, two were still in place. Two had been forced out. One couple, nervous about a confrontation, quit the house. Another couple stayed six months, and saved enough money to move onto an organic farm in the panhandle. They weren't quite storybook plots, but it did reflect some success, and his mission faced surprisingly little resistance from neighbors. A good part of it had to do with Rameau's criteria for who got placed into a home: families only, no individuals, and every family had to have at least some type of income, however small, in order to cover the power and water. He did not help the chronically homeless, or anyone with an addiction. This narrowed down his candidates considerably. "We feel kind of awful about the fact that we're making these distinctions," he said as he shut down his computer. "It worries me and bothers me and keeps me up, because one person really has no more right to that house than another." But they weren't in the business of social work, and he'd drawn a firm line between that and liberating homes. Plus, he was savvy enough to pick his battles. "If we move someone into a home and they fall into drug addiction," he said, "then the story is that we're opening up crack houses rather than moving people into homes. It confuses the issue."

Another reason for the largely sympathetic response to Take Back the Land's mission was that they stayed close to home, working mostly in Little Haiti and Liberty City, in poorer neighborhoods rather than forcing the experiment into places like Cutler Bay. But that, too, was part of the point. Max had a constituency. "We do work in the black community," he said. "So this is where I want to focus."

He had some scouting to do, and a computer to deliver, and he invited me along. I grabbed a monitor and followed him out to his car. The trunk was stuffed with clothes and bags and books. Inside, it was even more of a mess—empty water bottles, mail and maps stuffed in the door pockets, a toddler's car seat in the back, the flotsam of a hectic life. He cranked the engine, strapped his seat belt on, crammed a printout of addresses between the seat and hand brake, and checked for traffic. The street was empty. He let the hand brake down, then darted out onto the bright, wide street.

———

Miami is a Technicolor city, especially in neighborhoods like Liberty City and Little Haiti, where the architecture unfolds like a graphic novel of black culture and history, painted in storefront murals, across awnings and under overpasses. Buildings of almost every color—sky blue, pink, yellow, coral—are splashed with visages of Martin Luther King, Malcolm X, and Barack Obama. Barbershops have barbershop scenes painted on the storefront. Chitterlings, oxtail, wigs: What can be found inside is advertised without. Through a language painted in fits of color, in every breed of typeface, the city advertises a tough and vivid psyche.

Rameau moved to Little Haiti in 1993, after a stint at Florida International University (where, out of his intense and unusual fidelity to the disadvantaged, he dropped out just a few credits shy of a degree). As we drove through the neighborhood, past its murals and bodegas, he talked about the indignity of its gentrification in the late '90s, as it was splintered off into neighborhoods like Buena Vista and Morningside, a boom phase that led to the displacement of a considerable number of Haitian families. "Code Enforcement would go around giving tickets to people who didn't paint their houses frequently enough," he said, leaning to see the street numbers, looking for his turn. "They'd lien people's houses because they had chickens in the yard. These fines would balloon up to, say, two thousand dollars, and the families that had bought the place—two or three families who went in on it together—couldn't pay, so the city takes it over and kicks them out. And then some white couple comes in and buys the place."

He was passionate about the neighborhood. It kept him grounded. Max was born in Haiti, to wealthy parents—his father, who died in 1990, was an OB/GYN; his mother is a nurse—but moved to the United States when he was just three months old, when his father took a residency in Washington, D.C. Growing up in Maryland, Max spent summers in Haiti with his grandparents, where the disparity between his family's wealth and the country's poor fused with his maturing self-awareness, and got him thinking about the larger picture. "If you're in a particular position," he said as we were driving, "what are you doing to either make things better or ride things along? Given the fact that such an overwhelming number of people in that country are poor, and our family is not, what's the relationship between our family and the rest?"

Rameau, too, was forced out of his apartment as part of Little Haiti's gentrification, though he got lucky, buying a home in neighboring Allapatah for less than the cost of rent—the old-fashioned way of doing it. In response to this and other land-related issues in the black community, Rameau founded Take Back the Land, which launched its first experiment in the fall of 2006. Five years earlier, Miami-Dade County had razed a sixty-two-unit, low-income apartment complex in Liberty City, but never rebuilt—leaving hundreds homeless and the corner blighted. One late-October afternoon, Rameau and other volunteers raided the empty lot, building a shantytown out of pallets and plywood as the police surrounded them. Eventually the police backed down, and Umoja Village, as it was called, began to draw national attention. It was a radical move that provoked the umbrage of the city's officials and even its ministers. The idea of an American shantytown, especially one rising up on land usurped during the city's boom years, triggered surprising divisions. Umoja Village lasted six months before burning to the ground: officially, a cooking fire in one of the huts spread out of control, though Max wasn't altogether convinced it was an accident. In Miami, where housing had become such a surreal, dirty battleground, his suspicions didn't seem like much of a stretch.

But despite its brevity, Max considered Umoja Village a success. Not only did it provide food and shelter, it allowed, through a kind of utopian order, an autonomy for its residents that was otherwise well out of reach. "People who lived there made decisions about the rules of the place," he said. "For many people, for the first time, they had some level of control over their lives. They were actually participating in a democratic process in a way that had some meaning. That was the real thing that happened there, people were given some real level of dignity."

Seizing a neglected home involved two critical steps: One was to pore through court records and online sources, comparing addresses to deeds to weed out whatever properties didn't fit the criteria. "If it's owned by some old lady who lives a few miles away, or some schmuck in Ohio," Rameau said, "we don't take it over." They preferred capitalizing on the banks' log-jammed inventory, or whatever the city had sitting idle. (The house Take Back the Land controlled the longest—just over a year—wasn't even a foreclosure, but a public-housing unit the city had boarded up and ignored.) The other step was to *drive*: "Every street and every avenue. We write down the addresses of places that have potential. We go down, we look at it, we take notes."

This kind of scouting was critical, because it allowed Rameau to see up close what the data couldn't tell him: whether a roof leaked, or if the plumbing worked, or if rats had infested the place, or if the electrical wiring had been ripped out—whether a place was, by the rough standards of these circumstances, habitable.

We pulled up to a white-stucco two-bedroom with a narrow stoop. Max had liberated the house the year before, but the family was evicted after just four months. The house had been sitting empty since. On both sides of the front door, glass block rose to about the level of the doorknob and was topped by cheap aluminum windows encased in concrete—a repair job, and a sloppy one. One window was lower than the other, the lower one shaded by an awning, the higher one encased in a wrought-iron grill. Along the side of the house, more iron grills, but with plywood covering where glass should have been.

When the family lived here, Max said, all the windows were intact; the front ones were jalousies, shattered by vandals after the family was evicted. Vandals had preceded the family, too. Upon liberating the house, Take Back the Land covered holes in the walls where the copper had been ripped out. To make up for the damaged wiring, Serve the People, a sister organization, donated a small solar panel, which was planted on the roof to provide just enough power.

Max pointed to the tiny stoop, where white paint had dried on red tile steps. The week before the move-in, he dropped by to check on the place, and discovered that the couple moving in had already come and painted it. "They took pride in the fact that they were here," he said. "I'm not going to argue with you, they didn't do a great job, but I think it says something that they took the initiative. And at that point it became their house."

I followed him around as he inspected the place. Looking at it, he began to sound upset. "This is really infuriating," he said, "because that family could have been staying here. If you charged them two hundred dollars a month, the bank's going to break even. Right now they're losing a shitload of money. It's just sitting here empty. There's no one living in it, it's not doing anyone any good." He stared at it, repeating to himself. "This is doing *no one* any good, *no one's* living here. This is doing no one any good . . . what's the point?"

———

THE next day, the Dow would flutter between gains and losses, and close at just a hair above 7,500 points. Meanwhile, all eyes were on Phoenix, where Barack Obama was to unveil the $275 billion Homeowner Affordability and Stability Plan, the aim of which was to help 9 million homeowners who "played by the rules and acted responsibly" but nonetheless found themselves upside down on their mortgages.

Rameau, of course, thought the Phoenix speech was all much ado about the wrong thing. "The foreclosure crisis is not the problem," he said, craning his neck to see the street number. "It's a manifestation of the problem. They think the only thing wrong with the system is the housing crisis. It certainly is a way of making something that is obvious to me more obvious to everyone else." With every house—those we were after and those we happened to notice along the way—Rameau made fast, detailed notes, most of them scribbled in the car. And as he made his points, his train of thought would cause him to pull over, or miss a turn. His phone blinked, and he grabbed it to read a text message from his brother in Phoenix. "Hmph. My brother just met Obama." He jerked the car into a left-turn lane so he could turn around.

We pulled onto Forty-third Street, coasted down the block, but had trouble finding the house number. I saw one that had potential: small, stucco, sort of a Spanish colonial, beat-up but solid on the outside. From the street we could see over the low front patio, straight through the front windows to the kitchen in the back, and the yard beyond. Clearly it was empty.

"Plus, it's got a lockbox," I said.

"But the evens are on this side," Rameau said.

We looked up and down the street.

"They've all got lockboxes," I said.

He yanked the hand brake. "This is how it happens. We go to look for a place, and we find three."

We got out and walked over to an aqua-green cottage set behind a tall, white-rail fence, with a florid, wrought-iron screen door leaning off its hinges. The block was gritty but festive, lush with palms and oaks crowding Easter-colored bungalows. About a hundred yards away, I-95 soared behind a soundwall lined with more palms.

Max opened the gate. The Doberman next door spotted us, rushed up to its fence, and snapped and glared and made a vicious racket. I turned and could see more dogs down the street—collared, but big and loose, and roaming. I watched as they closed in on a mailwoman, who waited until they got just near enough before she whipped out a can of Mace and sprayed them with the clockwise efficiency of a sprinkler.

Auction signs were piled up near the ferns on the ground. Max ducked around the side to check the circuit breaker, found it, and fiddled with the wires. The electricity appeared to be intact. He seemed impressed. "This one's actually pretty good. I just need to see if it sold at that auction. I know it went to an auction, but I don't think it sold." He could see inside (it looked clean enough), but we couldn't find a way in. "Basically," he said, "I just need to get someone who's better at breaking and entering than I am. We have a couple of very thin people good for going through windows and stuff like that." We continued around the house, passing about a foot from the Doberman as it slobbered and barked. Max seemed nonplussed. When he'd made his way back to the stoop, he called the number on the sign. The house had been sold just that Sunday.

No worries: Two more foreclosures were across the street, the Spanish stucco included. Crossing over to it, we took a closer look, and just by what he could see through the windows Rameau knew it was unfit to squat. The patio was missing a roof. There were holes in the floor. The whole thing was a hazard. This house would remain the bank's problem.

The rest of the day was mixed: Most houses were too crippled for Max's purposes, unfit even to squat safely. We found plywood over windows and plywood where a front door should have been. One property, a government-owned duplex, was sealed tight with aluminum shutters, shutting out light and air: rats in there for sure, Max guessed. We discovered gutted air conditioners, stolen air conditioners; houses where the floor was missing; where lizards reigned; houses that looked brand new but were so small they were more like stucco huts.

Just inside the neighborhood of Allapatah, the yellow ranch-style foreclosure we were looking for had a FOR SALE sign out front, which wasn't necessarily a deterrent. We walked around back, where we found the sliding-glass door wide open. Max stepped inside, sang a soft "Hello?"

Whoever lost the house had been remodeling it. They'd put in granite countertops, and the cabinets looked new. But the walls were pocked with holes—someone seeking copper. The circuit breaker was missing; the water heater, too. Every appliance had been taken out, the place eviscerated. The only personal effect left was a poster of Lil' Kim taped next to the master bathroom.

"Thing is, you never know who took it," Max said of the

missing appliances. "Was it the agent? The homeowner? I know this lawyer, he has clients who get foreclosed on. He defends them in court, but once they lose the house, he sends his guys to take the appliances. I mean, he represents them in good faith, but once the house is empty he goes in and cleans it out."

He turned the faucet, the pipes gurgled. "We'd consider moving someone in," he said, though it would require putting up a solar panel. "That and we'd have to figure out if we can get the water running." Heat wafted down from a hole in the ceiling. "We'd cover up these holes," he said, pointing. "The solar panel wouldn't be enough to run a fridge or central air, which could be a huge problem in the summer. But there are people who live here without it anyway. We just have to see how the trees shade out." The solar panel would simply have to do. He'd call some volunteers together to complete what repairs they could; the family would do their part by cleaning.

We hit one last house before grabbing lunch, set back deep on what seemed like half the block, three lots at least. The fence was iron-rail, and tall. The house looked abandoned from a distance. Max was tempted to climb the fence, but was worried because of a bad knee. But we dug in, climbed it, and started shifting through the waist-high cattails and weeds. The neighbor girl was on the phone, watching, and hollered at us. "Hey! The people who own that house, she's been down the street. She just pulled out."

"Is she selling it?" Max asked her.

"I think her son trying to sell it."

"Is her name Zan something?"

"Huh?"

"Zan?"

She mumbled something like "Ahhhnom," and shook her

head and resumed her conversation on the cell. We high-stepped through the tall grass back toward the fence. Rameau paused, looking for another way out, and I jogged toward the neighbor's lot to see if there was a gap in the fence line, something to crawl through. But we were trapped. Max approached the railing with an embarrassed grimace. "Any kind of hopping and climbing through windows and stuff like that is just . . ." He let the sentence trail off and shook his head. "It's more than I usually like to do."

The next morning, Rameau was visited at his office by a family that had been evicted from a two-bedroom house on N.W. 137th Street. He already knew one of the family members—Mary Trody, who volunteered at the Miami Workers Center. Trody's mother, Carolyn Conley, owned the house. In November 2008, Trody and her husband, Antlee Accius, moved in with Conley, saying that their landlord had gone into foreclosure. Both Accius and Trody worked part-time, night shifts: Accius delivered copies of the *Miami Herald*; Trody stocked groceries at a Winn-Dixie. When they moved in with Conley, they brought a big family with them: their son, Sylvester, and daughters Annie and Mia. Mia herself was a mother of four, and brought along her boyfriend, Brandon. As of Friday afternoon, Conley was staying with her fiancé in a house without electricity and water; Trody's family had packed everything they could into a bread truck, which they now called home.

I found Max in front of the foreclosed house, a brittle, pale-gray, postwar ranch with wide vinyl siding. The house seemed to sag a little above the front door. Max slowly paced the yard amid the furniture the trash-out crew had set outside: a La-Z-Boy and ottoman, a couple of metal foldout chairs, a dresser, a microwave, and a couple of twin mattresses. Black garbage bags, stuffed with smaller possessions, lay on top of the furniture. In a day or so, according to county eviction codes, the trash-out crew would return to haul whatever wasn't salvaged, or stolen, off to the dump.

The yard was dry, the grass dead in spots. None of the family was there. Max made one phone call after another, planning a very public showdown for Monday morning, when he and other volunteers—armed with banners, pickets, and a bullhorn—would help move the Trodys back in, then stage a defense once the cops arrived to kick them out again. Reporters and cameras would be at the ready, from every media outlet Max could summon, every contact he had on file.

Something didn't feel quite right. I walked around the house, then looked back and realized the pattern of the scattered trash—bottles, cups, paper, pieces of the house—didn't fall into a radius that suggested a trash-out crew's work. The garbage was strewn in such a way that its reach and pattern suggested an abandon over time, a slow blight. I looked through the windows and saw a raw plywood floor; in every room, the carpet had been ripped out. I had seen hundreds of places like this. Each triggered its own combination of revulsion and pity and anger, and each required its own discipline to decipher and explain. What's left behind, in the way it falls or is tossed, is never just junk but a stroke of sorts—a mark, the chalk line around a body, the tags near the casings. Rameau's plan to move the Trodys back into this house was a first, since he usually liberated homes others had been evicted from, houses that had often been scavenged by the time he found them, so that whatever scars were found were those of strangers, often vandals. But here the garbage in the yard, the plywood floor, the general decay of the place was no one else's mark but that of the family who had owned it. Did the psychology of poverty explain it? As I looked up and down the street, none of what I saw reflected the same degree of degradation. Some homes were actually charming, well kept. Given one of the promises of Take Back the Land's mission—that, rather than let a foreclosure sit like an open target, a squatting family could protect its value, thus protecting the value of the neighborhood—I wondered if moving this family back into a home they had themselves ruined might make things a little more complicated. Conley had apparently lived here for over twenty years, and the family claimed an emotional attachment to the place, but was this the best scene around which to stage a spectacle?

A neighbor had been watching us, and walked over. "I own a landscaping business," he said. "So you guys, you know, if you need any help, you can call me up."

"We don't own the place," Rameau said quickly.

"They was here till last night," the neighbor said.

"Were they good neighbors?" I asked him. "Were they rowdy?" It was a leading question, but I thought it was important to know.

"Bad," he said. "That's where all of the trash comes from. Rowdy, rowdy, rowdy."

"Did you ever get into arguments about it?"

"Naw. I stay on my side. There was an older lady staying here. I don't know where she went."

"She's now staying in an empty house with no electricity," Rameau answered, with some force.

"I think it's a fair question to ask," I said. "Were they good neighbors? Maybe they were messy, but were they good neighbors?"

I could see Rameau tighten up at my interference.

"They were messy and loud, yeah," the neighbor said. "But that could be anybody." He pointed across the street. "The house there is loud, too."

"I still think it's two separate questions," Rameau said. "One is, 'Were they good neighbors?' The second is, 'Whether they were good neighbors or not, you have twelve people with nowhere to stay. What should be done?'"

The answer was obvious. The Trodys needed help.

"Just so you know," Rameau said to us. "I talked with them about this. I told them that if we move them back into this place, the ones who are going to keep them in the house—it isn't going to be me. It's going to be the neighbors. And that's the truth. If the media comes by here and everyone on camera is saying, 'Damn, they're loud,' or whatever, the police are going to come and everyone will be cheering. Conversely, if everyone says, 'These people have a right to be here, these people have nowhere else to go,' then it's going to be very difficult for them to be moved out. So I understand."

The neighbor got it. "I don't want to see no one homeless or anything like that," he said. And with a shaking of hands, he excused himself and went back to his side of the lawn.

I asked Rameau if any of the families he had helped had failed to live up to the social contract.

"There are people who have made a decision I wouldn't have made," he said.

A landscaping crew showed up at the foreclosure across the street, cranked up their blades and blowers, and went to work.

Max surveyed the yard, the house, taking it all in. He expected about a couple dozen supporters to show up on Monday, and for the crowd to thin out once the cops arrived. He and the core members would be prepared for a defense, which meant chaining themselves to the home.

I thought he was speaking figuratively. But then he led me to his car, where he opened the trunk and dug through his clothes and books and pulled out a gleaming quarter-inch chain fit to pull a car. A phrase looped in my head—*Junkyard Dog*—and I laughed nervously, skeptical.

If things went well, it would all make the news at six.

That evening, about a half-hour drive north, in Fort Lauderdale, hundreds of men and women began settling in to sleep overnight outside the county housing-authority building on Sunrise Boulevard, hoping to get a good spot for the next morning's distribution of applications for Section-8 housing. Three thousand applications were scheduled to be handed out. Flyers had been distributed explaining the process, with instructions not to arrive before seven the next morning, a Saturday.

Barricades were set up around dawn, closing off the block. By the time the housing authority started handing out applications, the crowd had swelled to about four thousand people; by 9 a.m. it had swelled to six thousand, most of them angry at the sluggish pace with which the county was running things, and frustrated by the realization that there were far more people than the county expected. Soon after the doors opened, the crowd's temper reached a pitch, and Fort Lauderdale police arrived and shut the scene down. It didn't spill over into a riot, but by most accounts it came very close. About 2,800 of the 3,000 applications were distributed. The first applicant could expect to hear back from the housing authority within six months; the 2,000th recipient was told to expect a call within three years.

Trody's family, meanwhile, spent the weekend living out of the bread truck, wherein they'd stuffed a couple of mattress, a small sofa, a television, and piles of clothes. A couple of years before, Trody had donated the truck to the Miami Workers Center, where she volunteered, to be used as a traveling gallery of photographs by residents of Wynwood, a largely Hispanic neighborhood. The name of that project, Galiería del Barrio, was still painted on the side.

I could see the blue-and-white truck, bright and battered, with that festive Spanish logo, as I pulled into a shopping center parking lot off Fifty-fourth Avenue. It sat at the far end, a bashful distance from the restaurant where Rameau and I were scheduled to meet the Trodys that afternoon, a Sunday. A film crew, dispatched the night before by director Michael Moore, had filmed them all at church that morning, and was now treating them to a Chinese buffet. Moore was assembling a documentary about the crisis—*Capitalism: A Love Story*—due out in the fall, and had learned about Monday's showdown through one of Max's supporters. The showdown seemed like the right opportunity to film. Now was a good time to map out a strategy.

The lunch was chaotic, but not panicky. Max and the film crew were gathered at one table, the family at another. Mary Trody was there, along with her son, Sylvester, and daughters Annie and Mia, whose four children, all toddlers, sat side by side. Her boyfriend, Brandon, sat across from her. I took an empty seat next to Trody, across from Conley. Accius had worked the night shift, and was sleeping in the truck.

Conley, injured after falling at a grocery store, had trouble getting around, and used a walker. I brought her a plate, and talked with her and Trody while they ate. Trody told me about her past, growing up in Miami, how she'd been at the *Herald* since she was just a girl. "I started when I was thirteen," she told me. "I worked a good five or six years with single-copy. When I turned nineteen I began working on the loading dock. I loved it. I loaded the trucks, drove a forklift." She said she stayed with the *Herald*, in one form or another, for thirty years, and afterward picked up work at the same Winn-Dixie where she'd delivered the paper. The *Herald* was something of a family tradition: Accius delivered papers for them, and Annie had spent the previous night helping him on his route. Mia added that she helped now and then. They all spoke of it with affection.

"My grandchildren were all raised at the *Herald*," Conley said.

Behind me, Rameau was going over logistics with Karen and Basel, the film's producers. Daniel, the cinematographer, sat at the end of the table. Rameau was thrilled by Moore's interest, but wanted to make sure he managed their access carefully.

"We're going to chat with the family about media stuff," he told the crew. "Just make sure there's no nerves, go over questions they might have, so that they're not a wreck tomorrow. It's going to be very stressful for them tomorrow."

Karen asked about what they could have access to, how deep they could go—film Max as he brainstormed with the Trodys, maybe eavesdrop on a call to the real estate agent, the same secrets I wanted to take notes on, the machinations of the event, how the gears wound and in which direction.

Daniel wanted access to the bread truck, but it was already clear that Trody wasn't comfortable with it.

"It's a *big* deal," Rameau said.

"To be inside that truck," Daniel said, "to feel it, that's really what the story is. It doesn't have teeth at this point."

They'd work on it. For now, the plan was to get back to Rameau's office, film the family arriving there, talking with him—taking instructions, establishing the relationship—and maybe if they were lucky they'd get a shot of the family slipping into the bread truck for the night. Some true grit.

The morning of the showdown, Max called and sent me to a house where Moore's crew was filming another eviction, one that had taken him by surprise. I pulled up to find Daniel filming a woman on the stoop. I'd find out later that he had tried to film the trash-out crew inside, but had been shoved out the door. I didn't realize at first how tense the situation was, or how rough the trash-out crew was, either.

The insides of the house were being dumped through a side door onto the grass. The small front yard was packed with furniture. Another woman was pacing the sidewalk in front of the house, hand on her hip, thrusting an arm at the trash-out crew and yelling to make damn sure that that man with the camera heard what she had to say. "See, they ass in there *stealing*!" she yelled. "That why y'all don't want the man out there on the field, 'cause they *stealing* shit! See, they ain't bring none of Roy's stuff out there yet! They ass in there stealing. Kiss my ass, bitch!"

The Roy she was talking about was the brother of the woman on the stoop. He appeared soon enough: a giant man, black, broad shouldered, thick, who projected the kind of calm only men his size possess. He betrayed no stress over this scene. I learned in listening to him that the house had been lost because of back taxes—a mistake, he said, because he'd already paid up. He kept making references to his lawyer, warning the camera that once she arrived with the paperwork a judge had signed, those trash-out boys would be putting all that stuff back inside.

I went around the side of the house, to where more furniture was piling up. They were sloppy about it. The crew, about five guys methodically slipping in and out through the kitchen door, all seemed in good spirits. One of them, dressed in a gray hoodie, set a pile of clothes on a dresser, and I asked him just how, exactly, he and the others had gotten this gig. Were they a company?

"Yeah, we a *company*," he said, frustrated, as if someone finally understood what he'd been trying to explain all morning. "Whoever owns the house now called us. They got the eviction downtown."

"I know how it works."

"Okay, *so*. We just don't come in nobody's house and throw they stuff out! You gotta get a order for this. The police done been here this morning. The police come with us and serve them they papers, and walk through the house, and check everything, tell 'em they gotta be outside, and find a way to get they stuff out."

"Who hires you?"

"Whoever owns the house."

"The bank?"

"The *bank*. The bank owns the house and whoever finance the house, through the people however that go."

"You have a company. A business card or anything."

A guy with a do-rag appeared in the doorway. "Man, get the

fuck out of here. I know what the fuck you trying to pull. Get the fuck out of here."

They started laughing.

"You know what *the fuck* you trying to do. You can't underplay me, man, get the fuck out of here, man."

"No, tell me. Seriously."

"No, get the fuck outa here, man!" Throwing an armful down, and with a dead stare, he turned and walked back inside, still talking at me. I heard a couple more voices laughing. I walked away.

At the front stoop I stopped and listened to Roy, who was explaining again how it would all play out. "Soon as my lawyer get here, with the judge's signature on it, they wind up putting it right back."

"Do you guys have any place you can put this right now?"

"No, we have nothing," the woman standing next to him said. She sat there in a daze. Daniel trained the camera on her for a long shot.

Roy's cell phone rang, and he walked toward the street and took the call. His sister answered Karen's questions, but mostly unraveled a convoluted indictment of the companies whose names appeared on all the paperwork, though she couldn't quite articulate what each had to do with the foreclosure. While she was talking, Roy walked back into the house, and I could hear the muddled bass of his voice from within, speaking calmly. He walked back out and stood next to his sister. A short while later, the man in the hoodie emerged with a computer monitor and set it gently on the stoop next to Roy, with sudden great respect for this item. That done, the whole crew emerged from the house, ambled across the yard, jumped in a truck, and drove away—without a word to Roy, and without placing a lockbox on the door. It was hard to tell if this was some last act of solidarity, or if they'd forgotten, or if their job was strictly to flush the house of all possessions and disappear. Either way, they didn't bother sticking around for the judge's signature.

A sparse crowd had gathered at Conley's house. Banners draped the windows—announcing the support of LIFFT (Low-Income Families Fighting Together) and the Miami Workers Center. A bedsheet with something stenciled on it lay atop the roof, but was illegible from the street. I spotted Trody, who was holding still while one of the film crew fiddled with her microphone battery. Reporters and cameramen huddled around to interview her, and she obliged them, but often interrupted herself when she saw a familiar face from the Workers Center, darting out of the circle of cameras to greet each one, hugs all around. The mood was festive, voices high.

Max paced up and down the sidewalk, made phone calls, took others, talked to cameramen, stayed on message. Nearly every local news station had sent a reporter, including GenTV, a Latino channel. Freelance writers and photographers were there with venues like the *New York Times* and *Mother Jones* in mind. Three calls were made to Chris Richards, the agent who was listed on the FOR SALE sign, to provoke him into coming down, or calling the police, or both.

Conley was seated, hands on her walker, talking to a cluster of cameras pressed in close. Trody, meanwhile, was delivering her own speech to other reporters. "Housing is a right," she said. "Housing is a *right*. All these rich people take these houses from here and nobody has a home. It's a right. They have no right to take homes from families and put 'em on the street."

Rameau steered the crowd into a circle around Trody and

Conley, and then Hashim Benford, an organizer with the Miami Workers Center, began to chant: "Say up with the people!"

Some folks shouted, "Yeah, yeah." Others repeated what he'd said. Benford stopped. "Say, 'yeah, yeah,'" he told the crowd, then began again . . .

"We're up with the people!"

"Yeah! Yeah!"

"Up with the people!"

"Yeah! Yeah!"

"Down with the banks!"

"Boom! Boom!"

"Those nasty banks!"

"Boom! Boom!"

Neighbors strolled past and paused, and kept their distance. The news-truck generators clicked on and grumbled.

One of Take Back the Land's members made her way to the center, for the introduction, and explained their mission. Benford followed with a few words, and then Trody was ushered toward them. She was nervous, and had a lot to say—too much, and too anxious; the speech didn't quite carry, but unwound in an awkward improvisation. "They have no business taking homes from God's people, they have no business taking homes. These are our babies, and then what's they's solution?"

People clapped, but weren't quite fired up.

Conley moved to the center of the circle. "This is my home," she said. "These banks and these people that sit behind the desk and say they gonna do this and do that, they need to come out here, come live on the streets for about a week or two and find out what it's like for the families! 'We're gonna do this, we're gonna do that.' No, you're not doing *nothin'* to help the families! All you doing is *separating* the families. We got places boarded up in projects and stuff. Why they boarded up? Why can't they come out and fix these places? And what's this with Section 8? You got to be perfect to get a Section 8? No, it ain't supposed to be like that. We're supposed to have a place to go. This is family. I believe in God almighty"—and here, the Lord invoked, the crowd was hooked, and it applauded, crisp and loud. Conley nursed the mood. "These people in the churches, listen to me. I know there's a God. Y'all watch TV. You watch everything underneath the sun. You talk, but you don't get out here *and fight*! I'm here to *fight*! Come fight! Fight with me! Make these banks come out and talk to you and find out what kind of income you can give them until you settle. Don't throw the people out. It's got to stop! Don't say you can do this for the community. I don't see nothing done in the community. I see people sleeping on the streets trying to figure out where their next meal is going to come from. Can't get a hot bath. Come on, y'all, you out there. I *know* you're out there. Stand up and fight! I'm sixty-six years old, and if I can stand here and fight, y'all can stand up and fight."

That did the job. The circle cheered, and then the cheering subsided for whoever was moved to speak next. But the pause stretched, and the circle remained empty, long enough to threaten the vibe and ruin the momentum. Would any of the kids speak?

Sylvester, Trody's son, walked shyly to the center. It was clear he didn't have his grandmother's fire-and-brimstone zing. He seemed introspective. "I'm one of the youngest people out here that is fighting for this house," he said, "for my mother and my grandmother. They're getting put out on the streets. I'm getting put out on the streets. What kind of life will I have being a child on the streets, just 'cause they want to take a house from us? This house was not perfect. It was not. But it was something

I could call a home. A roof I had over my head. Somewhere I take a shower every morning and eat every night. And they just want to take it away from us, and put us on the streets? That is not right. That's not right for nobody. Nobody should see their parents go through this kind of pain. Nobody should see a child like me go through this kind of pain. At such a young age. And I know what it's like to be in the real world—" And then he stopped, as if he'd run out of anything else to say. The applause was tepid.

Rameau moved to the center, reiterated Take Back the Land's philosophy, then looked at the house. "So on behalf of this family and this community, we liberate this home for this family."

The crowd cheered again, and slowly people began picking up the furniture and moving it inside, to chants and songs of community power.

By late morning, the mood was joyous, the activists singing, elders chatting in lawn chairs in the front yard. There was more a spirit of celebration than revolution. I spotted Max on the sidewalk, surrounded by a cluster of cameras. A reporter was interviewing him, and they'd landed on the obvious question.

"Where do you draw the line, though," the reporter asked, "if you have a person who is just irresponsible, and couldn't pay their rent—"

"We think that housing is a human right," Max interrupted, "and as a human right it really doesn't matter if the person is responsible or irresponsible or whatever. Every human being by virtue of their own humanity has a right to housing. I think George W. Bush is extremely irresponsible. He never lost his housing because he has a wealthy father. And we think this family deserves at least the same breaks that George W. Bush got."

The reporter brought him back. "So do you want to see some laws changed? Because regardless of what you're saying, it's still the law. They're still breaking the law."

"Not all laws are right," Max said. "So I'm not going to fight for laws, which are just man-made constructs, when there's a bigger—something a little higher than the laws."

The reporter wasn't satisfied. "We've done this story on you before," he said, "and we got a lot of e-mails from people saying you should be arrested, that this is illegal. That you're not above the law. Laws are still factual whether you agree with them or not."

"I think someone should be arrested for this," Max said, "but it shouldn't be me and it shouldn't be the family. It should be the crooks who are responsible for this economic housing crisis. Those are the people who should be arrested for doing this."

"But not everyone is in a situation where it was fraud related. Some people, you have to admit *some* responsibility. They get these mortgages from the banks, they can't afford them, and when the property is foreclosed, they don't have—"

"If they get the mortgages from the banks and they can't afford it, that means the *bank* is being irresponsible, irresponsible in the lending. The primary responsibility goes to the bank. I'm not going to lend my money to you if I don't think you can pay me back—"

"But if I ask for a loan knowing I can't pay for it, do I not have some responsibility for that?"

"I think you have the exact same responsibility as the bank has for giving the loan. If you come to me and you say you need money because you have *no* money and you have *no* job, and I *give* you the money, fully expecting to get it back? It's just as much on me as it is on you. Just for the record, if you ask me for money, I'm not going to give it to you unless you think you can get my money back."

The reporter didn't laugh.

Max picked up again: "If you're going to have arrests around this crisis, the arrests should start with the worst offenders, not the least offenders. And the worst offenders, I think, are the banks. Instead, what's happening in society is, instead of putting police toward the mass murderers, the police are being spent on people who are stealing candy from the corner store, and that is a bad use of society's money."

They risked talking past each other, and so I interrupted: "At what point is your job done with this house?"

"I don't know, I'm not really sure how to answer that. We don't have a set timeline."

"So if they call you next week and say, 'We're out,' does this start all over again?"

He didn't hesitate: "Yes."

Friday's eviction had been carried out with the help of a foreclosure-services company called Velozik Enterprises, a crew of about three men, including Chris Velozik, the company's owner, who was trim and tan and white-haired, wearing a company T-shirt—"SPECIALIZING IN FORECLOSURE SERVICES"—as he and his crew arrived that afternoon. I could see the bulge of a pistol holster underneath his T-shirt. He was returning to Conley's house to recover whatever furniture had been left behind after Friday's eviction and haul it off to the dump. He'd been backed up all weekend and couldn't get around to it until now, when he pulled up with truck and trailer to find a couple dozen people gathered in Conley's front yard, the furniture back inside. If he was surprised, he didn't show it. He simply walked up to the door, a clipboard tucked in his arm, surveyed the crowd, then told everyone it was time to go.

Max appeared, walking up to the stoop. He insisted Velozik reconsider.

Velozik clasped his hands near his belt buckle, nodded. "Let me tell you something," he said to Rameau. "The bank offered them—the realtor offered them—two thousand dollars to give them money to rent a place. They said no."

"Right now they are living in a truck," Max said. "This place is *empty*. There's an empty house over there, which is in much better condition. That house is going to sell way before this one."

"That's not my problem, sir. If the bank permits you to go inside—"

"The bank isn't making any money by this unit staying empty and this family being homeless," Max said. "They're not making *any money*. So call them and let them know what the humanitarian thing to do is."

Of course, Velozik had about as good a chance of reaching someone at the bank as Rameau did, but he didn't bother clarifying this point. "I work for the bank," he said. "They tell me to do the job. If I don't do it, they'll find somebody else to do it."

"May I say something," one woman asked, and began pointing out the value of empty houses and their depreciative effect on a neighborhood. It triggered a dozen points people had been ready all morning to make, and Velozik, with his hands clasped in front of him, tried to counter each one, a free-market logic countering the humanitarian logic of the crowd. The tension thickened.

Finally, Mia, Trody's daughter, boiled over. "You the bank!" she shouted. "It's not right that she's been in this house for twenty-two years and y'all going to put her out. It's not right! And you come in here saying that we're trespassing? We should be telling you that you trespassing, because this is *our house*! All this stuff that's going on in this house, you don't know what's going on in this house. She brung us up in this house!"

"I got a question," one man said. "Where is the money the federal government put in the banks? Where is that money?"

"Why don't you ask Obama?" Velozik said. He'd lost his poise.

The crowd howled at him.

"I'm asking *you* because *you* represent the bank! Where is the money Obama or whatever put in the hands of bank!"

Velozik kept quiet.

"You cannot answer?"

"Ask the bank," he said.

They howled again.

"*You* is the bank," Mia said. "That's what you said. So why you here representing the bank if you can't even answer the question!"

"The bank wants the property back."

"Want it back? For what! For it to sit on the block! For what? They gonna come here, and they gonna tear the frame out the windows, and it's going to be a piece of dust before tomorrow. Talking about you want the house back—for what? It's sitting here empty! Do you have a heart? Think about it, do you have a heart? Kids got nowhere to go, and you sittin here telling us the bank wants this property back! To sit here empty like this house, that house two houses down the street, and the one over here!"

Conley struggled forward, toward the stoop. "Do you know who God is? Do you go to church? Answer me!"

"Sure."

"You believe in God, you do? Does the bank believe in God?"

"Who financed the house for you?" Velozik asked her.

"Option One," she said.

"Have you spoken to them? What have they told you?"

"I've done everything I can," Conley said.

"Did you respond to their letters?"

"I done everything I can."

"Okay, what did you offer them and what did they offer you?"

"I tried to do a reverse mortgage."

Mia shouted, "She was ripped off! It was a predatory lender! She got *ripped off*!"

"I had people come in here and say they gonna do a reverse mortgage," Conley said. "I was all for that. I signed papers. They tell me everything is fine. They tell me I can live here the rest of my life, just pay the taxes. The next thing I get is these foreclosure notices. What kind of deal is that? Get out from behind your desk and come out here and talk to the people."

"And did they? They didn't make arrangements?"

"They didn't make nothing with her," Mia said. "This is what I'm telling you. This is why when the foreclosure notices came, everybody was sitting there in shock."

Conley sighed. "I know I can't read and write good," she said, subdued now. "Come on, I know my education. And I'm finding out now that people are out here taking advantage of people."

"I don't have a choice," Velozik said. He pulled out his cell phone and called the police.

The crowd launched into a chant.

In a fundamental way, this showdown on 137th Street was a crossroads moment, a knotting together of disparate philosophies—economics and ethics, culpability and forgiveness, merit and charity. There was a battle line, and where you stood suggested the American principle you believed in. In the air were arguments for both the meritocrats and the bleeding hearts. The problem was that if you agreed with the merito-cratic principle, you came up short with an appropriate fate for those who failed—or refused—to do their part. Was homeless-ness a fitting punishment? Starvation on the street?

Court records show that Conley borrowed $119,000 against the house in 2005, and that a *lis pendens* (the motion that begins a foreclosure process) was issued in March 2007. It remains unclear what happened to the money, apart from what the siding repairs sucked up. Whatever happened, there was hardly any evidence that the money had done any good. What was obvious to a lot of people in the yard that day, supporters and detractors alike, was that the house could never have reasonably been worth what was borrowed against it—no matter the appraiser's opinion, or, more likely, because of it. Conley claimed not to have seen any of the money promised her through the reverse mortgage's plan. She claimed to have none of the original paperwork, either. And all court records show was that the money was borrowed and never paid back. She could very well have been the victim of fraud, or could just as easily have spent the money. No one other than Conley and the broker she dealt with knew the truth.

Reporters followed Velozik as he walked away from the stoop and back to his truck, and once he'd put a few tools away, since this job would be on hold for a while, he took a few questions, hands clasped by his buckle, very cool-headed, trying to clarify the bank's position, though he only seemed to reinforce Rameau's point. "The bank doesn't want the houses," he said to us. "I want you to understand that. They don't want the houses. They want people to pay. They're in business to *sell* houses, and to get money from the principal and interest. But people don't want to pay. When it comes to this point," he said, nodding at the action on the lawn, "it's been many, many, many months. The bank offered them *two thousand dollars*. With two thousand, you can go and rent a place."

"How many houses have you trashed out?" I asked him.

"Thousands," he said. "I've done about six or seven hundred evictions since about three years ago. I go anywhere in Miami-Dade County."

"How long have you been at it?"

"About three years."

"What were you doing before that?"

"I invested in real estate."

The emotional watershed Velozik provided was enough to carry the crowd for a little while, for an hour or so after he'd left. But then the day began to stretch, until even the chants and songs had petered out. "Can you believe the police response times around here?" Rameau said, chuckling. "Unbelievable." He was lying on the grass, propped up on an elbow next to a starved-looking cypress stripped of its bark. He snatched a handful of grass and watched the blades drop. He was falling into a mood, a lighthearted brooding, a little nervous and irritated by the waiting.

Six patrol cars pulled up across the street, each lining up behind the other. Velozik returned, too, parking on the other end of the block and walking past the protesters to meet the police. They talked out of earshot, about twenty yards away. By then, the Trodys and everyone else were gathered in the front yard, the chanting clear and full-throated. Max stood close to Trody, and when one officer—middle-aged, burly, buzzcut—tried to coax her away from the crowd, toward his car, Rameau stepped in. "We don't want to have her isolated," he told the officer.

The officer paused, looked at him and thickened with tension. "Well, *you're* not in charge here," he snapped.

Rameau turned to Trody. "You don't have to say anything," he told her.

The officer turned on him. "Do I have to repeat myself to you? *You're not in charge.* We'll speak with her. We'll explain the law. And you're not going to decide whether or not she comes back with me, you understand? Do you understand what I'm saying? Do you understand what I'm saying? You are not in charge." Rameau kept chattering underneath this warning, and the more he talked the harder the officer spoke back at him, escalating, the air getting a little thick in that corner of the yard, until finally Rameau stopped and Trody walked away with the officer, taking his questions, muttering back.

As they were talking, a small woman named Poncho approached them. She was one of Take Back the Land's core five, the group's police liaison in case of a situation like this one, and now, taking her cue, she began speaking to the officer in a measured way that was soft but not condescending, almost breezy. In her disarming tone she provided the details Trody wouldn't, which seemed to satisfy the officer a little. They arrived at around eleven that morning, she said, and the doors were not locked when they showed up. They called the realtor to let him know what they were up to. And besides, everything that took place on the property that day had been captured by the cameras.

"Did you see any legal notices on the door?" the officer asked her.

"No."

"There weren't legal notices on the door?" he repeated.

"No, sir, not on the door. And I don't want there to be any misconceptions. We're not trying to hide or be sneaky."

"Obviously not," he said.

He walked off, the cops huddled. After a while he walked back up the block to tell Velozik he was free to file a report, and that was it. It made little sense to arrest a grandmother and her entire family in front of the local news, and of course everyone knew as much, but we all suspected they'd be back after the eleven o'clock report. That would be the best time to make their move, between midnight and the morning news. Max knew as much, and as soon as the patrol cars pulled away he began calling commissioners, the police chief, the mayor's office, whomever he could to try and win some promise of mercy for the Trodys, that they not be thrown out overnight.

Afternoon dragged toward evening; the crowd thinned out. Unmarked cruisers rolled past on the hour. By nightfall Mia's children arrived. Only Moore's crew and a couple of news trucks remained. Rameau waited, called, waited, and finally he caught a break: A police captain he knew offered to speak with Chief John Timoney, to ask that the family be allowed to stay the night. Max was beaming; the gesture alone was a victory. "It doesn't necessarily mean they're going to let you stay here long," he told Trody. "But that's the first step." They were all gathered in the living room as he said it, and were quiet. In a few hours, Trody would begin the night shift at Winn-Dixie. She was leaning back in a recliner, and looked spent. Max touched her shoulder. "I really need you to take a nap," he said. Leaning forward, she began to weep, almost winnowing in the seat.

Out in the dark again, heading home, I helped Poncho remove Take Back the Land's banner from atop the bread truck, climbing onto the hood to untie it. A wind was picking up, whipping the banner as it came loose. I jumped back down and handed her the other end of the banner, then slipped away to my own car to sit and watch the scene. Poncho wrestled with the banner, which the wind had pried from her. The Channel 10 van's lamps clicked off, its generator falling quiet. Then I saw Trody, blanket in hand, too nervous to sleep in the house, creep out the front door and back into the bread truck, just in case.

The next day, waiting in the car, watching cops cruise slowly past, I asked Max what it was in him, or in his past, that led to this kind of commitment.

"To be honest with you, I don't know. I lived a very privileged life. The day I turned sixteen I had a car—though I had to share it with my brother. I've never suffered police brutality. I just don't know what it is. My mother tells a story of when I was a kid. We went into town in Haiti and she bought me a piece of candy from a street vendor, and I demanded we buy something from every vendor because it wasn't fair we gave money to this person but not to the other one."

"So you do believe in the free market."

He laughed. "Well, I was just trying to redistribute my mother's wealth."

I remembered his argument with the reporter the day before, and what he'd said about trespassing laws, and how flippant he seemed. It bugged me. I sensed an intelligence in him, of course, but still couldn't peg him, still couldn't tell who, exactly, I was writing about, a revolutionary or a knee-jerk Marxist. For one thing, Rameau was a homeowner, a father, and a husband, and by default must have appreciated the protection the laws provided his family and his property. Obviously, he knew the value of privacy.

"I'd concede that the nuance wasn't in what I told that reporter," he said, "but that *overall* the statement was true. Where the nuance is missing is in distinguishing between a place where someone lives and an empty place that a corporation owns. And I think these laws really are intended to protect corporations at the harm of individuals who need places to stay. I think these laws are perfectly reasonable for the house twenty feet away from this one," he said, pointing across the street, then pointing back at Conley's house, "but here trespassing laws are providing the *exact* same protection to a corporation—*to a piece of paper*—as to human beings. And I don't think that's right. And I'm not even saying there should be *no* protections for corporations, but I definitely don't think the protections for corporations should be identical to the protections for human beings."

Was he worried that the living conditions in Conley's house—the plywood floors, the dirt, the missing bathroom sink, all of it broadcast now on local news—might undermine his cause?

He reminded me that I was witnessing an anomaly among the nine liberations so far. "This is not a good situation," he said. "The only thing worse than this family living here is this family living in the van. I think this is a horrible situation, I wish it wasn't like this. I've had my moments of doubt. And the only thing that has kept pushing me is thinking that this family is going to be back in that van. I just can't imagine that."

He looked at his watch: It was time to go. He slipped out, shut the door. I watched him drift down the sidewalk as he dialed a number, head low. The wind whipped his shirt a little. The Channel 10 crew had grown restless. They loaded up the van, lurched onto the street, then pulled away. A photographer, a woman, three cameras dangling by straps, approached the

Trodys' bread truck. She cocked her head, spoke, and gestured delicately, then climbed up and disappeared inside. A cat, stretched out in the middle of the street, watched her, then rolled over. The block was quiet, the sky sharp-blue and cloud-spotted. The cat scrambled: another unmarked cruiser rolling by, another pair of eyes behind the tinted glass, making the whole department's presence felt, punctuated by how it took the corner: pausing, then turning, then crawling out of sight, menacingly slow, infinitely patient.

Over the next several weeks, the police hovered but mostly kept their distance from the Trodys, driving past the house now and then just to make a presence felt. Winter turned to spring, spring to summer, and with the summer came an upswing: The Dow regained several months' worth of losses, cresting just above 9,500 points; new-home sales increased in several cities, after prices had flattened out in the spring; JPMorgan Chase and Goldman Sachs reported record profits; Bank of America and Citigroup followed suit, but reported profits that were much more transparent as a one-time gain from downsizing that winter.

Foreclosures, meanwhile, were holding steady, with a shadow inventory of homes swelling behind those sitting idle and for sale. Mortgage relief proved hard to come by; banks remained skittish about making loans to new buyers, even to buyers with stellar credit. With any gains in home sales, one had to wonder, given the banks' insistence on cash-only transactions, if the speculators were actually the ones bringing the market back to life, buying foreclosures outright, and cheap, so they could play lender to the leagues of people who wanted a first home, or a second chance.

Relief was nowhere near the level the Obama administration had promised in February. June's estimate of underwater mortgages in Florida stood at 45 percent, just over 2 million. Mortgage holding companies, meanwhile, had been collecting substantial fees from letting foreclosures drag out—profiting, in other words, from a homeowner's inability to modify a troubled loan.

And the homeless were growing in need and number. In June, Miami had the fourth-highest number of properties, nationwide—homes, condos, businesses—that received a foreclosure notice, and odds were that a considerable portion of the names on those notices would be appearing on a growing waiting list for affordable housing in Miami, which by summer stood at 70,000 strong.

In April, the *New York Times* ran a front-page story about Take Back the Land, based on the showdown at the Trodys' house. ABC visited next; the BBC followed. By the time I returned to Miami in late June, NBC was knocking on the door. Mary Trody and Carolyn Conley were both suffering from what Max called "media fatigue." He'd expected as much. During its first wave of attention from the press, Take Back the Land's go-to case was a doctoral student, a single mother of four who'd been abandoned by her husband. She was an immigrant, articulate, and the house looked spotless in every shot. She was, in many ways, an ideal ambassador of the mission. Eventually, the pressure of reporters became maddening. It is a lot to ask of people piecing their lives back together to expose themselves to the camera's bright ogling, week after week. It sapped an energy otherwise better spent. Soon she refused to participate in interviews. Now Trody was close to doing the same. And the camera crews kept lining up—Swedish television, French television, Australian, Japanese, and German. "The ethical dilemma is that I *need* to do the media part," Max said. "I actually want to turn them out to the media all the time, and do well, and perform well. And yet I have an obligation to protect them, even though protecting them doesn't move history."

Max, too, was close to burning out. When I caught up with him in the summer, he'd just returned from a frenzied schedule of cross-country lectures. He'd even squeezed in a tour of Gaza. During his weeks at home, he said, he was struggling to make ends meet. To that end, he'd been devoting less time to Take Back the Land and more time to the computer work that had gotten him through his early activist years.

But there was progress. Early in the summer, he'd been invited to an informal roundtable by Miami–Dade County Commissioner Katy Sorenson, who paired him with Judge Jennifer Bailey and Arden Shank, of Neighborhood Housing Services, to try and brainstorm a strategy and, as Sorenson put it, "to figure out if there's a way to go legal with all this stuff, figure out how to take an outlaw activity and make it a sanctioned activity that involves institutions and would benefit the whole community." No statutes were expected, but at least they could draft an informal policy that would allow banks and housing nonprofits to work together. Rameau was happy to trade ideas, he told me, but not at all interested in playing a subtler role. Politics wasn't his arena. He preferred the action on the ground.

To that end, he was busy planning Take Back the Land's growth on two fronts: "Locally, we're going to start working on defenses instead of liberations," he said, which was no less risky a tactic—technically, it's still trespassing—but stood to draw greater public support, since it worked to keep families in their own homes, approaching homelessness at the source. But he wasn't abandoning liberations altogether; rather, he wanted to see Take Back the Land's model replicated in other cities. "The big question is, can we do enough liberations to force the debate in something other than an abstract way, and say, 'Look: Right now, numerous organizations across the United States have control of over fifty thousand houses—what are you going to do now?' Right now, we're just not in a position to negotiate."

Fifty thousand houses sounded like an extremely ambitious, if not fantastical, number. But ACORN and New York's Picture the Homeless had already taken a page from Rameau's book, breaking into foreclosures and squatting on private empty lots, with arrests to show for it.

But the legal ramifications of such guerilla solutions—however much a family might have promised or intended to care for an abandoned foreclosure—made the odds very long on getting the banks to cooperate. Despite the economic advantages of having foreclosures occupied and tended, the banks simply were not in the property-management business.

The trouble was breaking through the Byzantine structure of the banks themselves. It took until the summer of 2009 for most to begin hiring and training enough agents to handle modifications; there was no telling how deep overstock was and whether the difficulty in filling those foreclosures was a matter of the overwhelming work at hand or a stubborn faith in free-market forces. Never mind that some banks were walking away from properties altogether—a phenomenon known as "bank walkaways," in which homeowners often left after receiving fore-closure papers, only to discover months later that the bank, hav-ing determined that the property simply wasn't worth the cost or trouble, skipped the courthouse auction and never actually foreclosed, leaving the home in legal limbo, with code violations piling up in the vanquished owner's name. These were houses no one wanted anymore, in legal suspension, ripe for taking up.

If only Max could figure out which ones were up for grabs . . .

Our last drive together, Max and I took another tour of the city, heading out along Twelfth Avenue, passing the "segregation wall"—a foot-high remnant of what was once a six-foot-high barrier demarcating Miami's black neighborhoods (Max was helping to organize a petition to make the wall a historical marker), up to Seventy-fifth Street, to the house he'd shown me last winter, where the jalousie windows had been shattered and so poorly substituted. Once there, we got out and kicked around. Pipes spilled out from a crawl space where the plumbing had been scavenged in the months since our first visit. The house next door was also now a foreclosure. We peeked through the front window, and could see black stains where squatters had tried to start a fire during a cold spell.

We shot over to N.E. Second Avenue, turning south toward downtown. Second Avenue offers an epic, sweeping perspective of the city, running straight from the ghetto toward the bay's glamorous towers, through Little Haiti and Buena Vista, past the savvy Design District, and into the heart of downtown. History lay all along this strip.

"At what point would you consider your mission accomplished?" I asked him

"When we don't have any more people coming to us," he said, smiling, and acknowledged that it wasn't going to happen anytime soon, "mainly because we don't have critical mass. If Miami were doing twenty move-ins a month, with ten different organizations, then I think it would happen. Critical mass would overwhelm the system."

Perhaps, but there was also the potential of crossing over into other neighborhoods, where his liberations would have a different social impact. "If you keep this in Liberty City," I suggested, "you're probably not going to get the kind of contentious debate you want." Would he rather create an even bigger stir in mostly white, middle-class subdivisions like Cutler Bay and Pinecrest?

"If we go into Culter Bay," he said, "do we move in a white family? Because we don't want to have to knock down two walls at the same time. If we're going into neighborhoods now and the neighbors support what we're doing—even if there's some trepidation—going into a white neighborhood and moving in a low-income black family just confuses the issue. We won't know whether they are opposed to the family because of race or class, and it doesn't help us in improving our own communities. We'd be out doing this in other communities, so there's not really any benefit."

All that said, there was something he wanted to show me. We headed east, then turned onto Bayshore Drive, cruising up to Morningside, an upscale neighborhood of Jazz Age mansions and one of the city's most scenic public parks, but where, during the boom, the streets along Bayshore were redesigned to create a bit more privacy.

"When I lived here," Max said, pointing to the landscaped berms, "these didn't exist. You can't go through here now because of this big planter. That didn't used to be there. And there was no guard gate."

As we approached the gate, I slowed into a U-turn.

"Keep going!" he said.

"We can go through?"

"Yeah! See the reaction you had?"

I rolled the window down as I slipped through the gate, but the guard ignored me.

"You don't have to put the window down, you don't have to explain anything," Max said, as incredulous as if he'd just discovered this secret. "It's a public road. But now that they put that guard gate there, all the Haitian families that used to come here make U-turns and leave, which is exactly what they wanted."

The neighborhood was thick with palms and other trees of an almost prehistoric grandeur. I could see the bay glimmering between the shrubbery. Then Max asked me to turn into what looked like an empty overgrown lot. I rolled over the carpet of fronds and small branches, then saw it: a red, sprawling stucco house, set back at the end of a curving brick driveway buried under the tarp of leaves, nearly swallowed by the trees and vines that surrounded it. It bespoke lost aristocracy and, shrouded as it was, had an archaeological vibe.

It began to rain, at first a drizzle, then a downpour loud and full. The drops were big, snapping a loud drumline on the truck's roof. We scrambled out into the downpour and crossed the courtyard to peek through the front-door glass. The house was empty, just a cream tile floor and white walls and sliding-glass doors that revealed Biscayne Bay in the close distance. A family of twelve could fit in here for sure, or two families of six, or who knows how many combinations, very comfortably. I imagined a utopian scene.

We picked through the overgrowth around the side, ducked past the brick grill, and made our way onto a wide back lawn that stretched toward the water, with a clear panorama of the bay and Miami Beach beyond. Suddenly the storm was a broad show; I felt the God-drenched zen found in seaboard vistas, a humility in the face of nature. I could imagine shaking off many troubles staring out at this sea, in rains like this one.

"So talk about taking this thing to the next step," Max said, grinning. "This would be the place to do it."

I had to admit it was a hell of a view.

PAPER

BARONS

———

Honeymooning in Miami Beach was my father's idea; my mother, impressed by an ad she'd seen of newlyweds canoodling in a heart-shaped tub—wrapped in bubbles, champagne in hand, rose petals scattered around candles on the floor—thought the Poconos would be nice. My father thought the tub was tacky; plus, the wedding was set for just after Columbus Day, and as beautiful as autumn's colors were in upstate Pennsylvania, October nights often slipped toward freezing. My parents had already spent three winters in Philadelphia and were due to spend another. Miami Beach offered a respite. The only problem was flying there, the risk of a hijacking, a reasonable fear in 1969. Eighty-two planes were hijacked in the United States that year, a good number of them landing in Havana. My father still wasn't naturalized as an American citizen, was still a refugee, and he worried that if their honeymoon flight was hijacked to Havana, that once the Cuban government discovered he was back on native soil, he'd be forced to stay. Such was the tenor of political gestures across the Straits.

The solution was simple enough, and in retrospect speaks to the innocence of flying then. He paid cash for the ticket, then provided the airline with another name, posing as my mother's brother Arnold. Airline tickets were issued nameless in the 1960s; the only reason an airline required a name at all was for a master list of passengers, used in worst-case scenarios to identify the dead. This time the flight landed safely, no worries, hardly a bump, and on October 18, 1969, Franny and Arnold Picón arrived at Miami International for a family vacation.

By then, Miami Beach was entering its doldrums. For nearly fifty years a hot streak of hotel building had made the shore itself a showpiece, beginning with such Jazz Age palaces as the Flamingo Hotel, the Wofford, the Roney Plaza, the streak working north over the decades, devouring the beachfront, peaking in the 1950s with the gaudy, fantastical mega hotels of Morris Lapidus, the Fontainebleau and Eden Roc in particular, for which developers Ben Novack and Harry Mufson spent millions trying to outdo each other's extravagances—in the lobby, in the ballrooms, down to the waiters' attire. The unhinged aesthetics made "the Florida style" infamous by the end of the '60s, and alarmingly popular (Lapidus would later put his stamp on buildings in Washington, Puerto Rico, and England). But however shocking the décor was, the spirit of grandeur was the same as it was in 1920, when Carl Fisher, a manic Hoosier entrepreneur, touched the boom off. It was all rooted in a simple equation that transcended generations of architects and tourists alike, articulated by one of Lapidus's contemporaries in 1965—namely, "to convince the sucker who's spending fifty bucks a day that he's really spending a hundred bucks a day."

Fisher, inventor of the Prest-O-Lite head lamp, founder of the

Indianapolis 500, father of the Lincoln Highway (the first trans-
continental highway in America) and the Dixie Highway (the
first cross-country highway to run north–south), discovered
this barrier island on vacation, sailing the bay, spotting a couple
of fragile outposts in the thick of what was mostly jungle. He
pulled ashore and went to have a look, and there met a man
named John Collins, a Jersey horticulturalist who'd been struggling on two fronts: to convert half his land into an avocado
grove, and convert the rest into a resort. A couple of bathing
pavilions, known as "casinos," already drew a small crowd, but
by ferry only. Collins had spent all his money building a driv-
able bridge from the mainland to the island, but went broke just
halfway across the bay. Fisher was a quick study, and didn't need
much convincing beyond the effects of a turquoise surf to see
what Collins saw, and with millions at his disposal, and being
the hyperactive sort, he quickly struck a deal with Collins, lending him enough money (with interest) to finish the bridge in
exchange for two hundred acres. In 1913, Collins got his money,
and Fisher got his land.

The two hundred acres was an almost impenetrable knot
of mangroves and palmetto, a sanctuary for exotic fauna—
alligators by the hundreds, small bears, wildcats, coral snakes,
rattlesnakes, rats, crabs, rabbits, and bugs (lots of bugs, enough
sand fleas and mosquitoes to bleed a man into a deep sleep). But
mostly, it was the land that put up a fight. Fisher attacked it with
everything at hand—men with machetes, dredgers, threshers he
had built for the very purpose of chopping through these leg-
sized roots. The story of Miami Beach is, in essence, the story
of a wealthy man's obsession versus an intractable vegetation.
What he couldn't yank out of the ground he burned, and what
was left over he buried, dredging tons of white sand from the

bottom of Biscayne Bay to be regurgitated on top of whatever stubborn growth or stumps could still be seen. Fisher dredged relentlessly (as Will Rogers put it, he made the dredger "the national emblem of Florida"), until the thickets disappeared, until the beaches strewn with seaweed and mophead dregs were buried under tamer, cleaner beaches. In a few months' time, nothing poked out of the sand without a purpose, some role in the big vision.

In 1915 the old sandbar became a city: five hundred residents, one paved road, and a small hotel, the Brown (two stories, pine and stucco, thirty-six rooms). Fisher, a natural promoter, began to push the island with every creative weapon he could devise, first to the middle-class "tin can tourists"—clattering down the Dixie Highway in Model Ts to access the vistas of the rich—then to the rich. He branded Miami Beach with a carnivalesque sex appeal through goofy, tantalizing ads of pin-up girls in tight bathing suits by the ocean (laughing, legs high); he enlisted an elephant, which sat for posing flappers and even caddied for Warren Harding. For good measure, Fisher rented a billboard in Times Square to remind New Yorkers in December that "It's June in Miami."

In 1920 he built the beach's first colossus, the Flamingo Hotel. A million and a half dollars got him eleven stories, two hundred rooms, a handful of private cottages, and a lighted dome that glowed on winter nights like a candy-colored lighthouse lamp. In the afternoons, tea dances packed the lawn, and there would have been actual flamingoes among the crowds had the entire imported flock not died en route (murals and statuettes would have to suffice). The imported polo players, on the other hand, thrived, adding starpower to the polo grounds he'd built. But even that wasn't enough. Something must have seemed too uniform about this fantasy, so, as a finishing touch, Fisher added a handful of gondolas (six built in twenty days), piloted by "some of the most wonderful Bahama negroes you ever saw to push these gondolas around. They are all going to be stripped to the waist and wear big brass ear rings. And possibly necklaces of live crabs or crawfish." For Fisher, no expression of his wealth was too ridiculous. As historian Howard Kleinberg noted, the Flamingo Hotel was both the turning point and the guiding principle, opulence where just a few years before the ocean beach had been a rat-infested jungle. In building the Flamingo, Fisher built the touchstone of the excess that would follow.

By the peak of speculation in Florida, just before the hurricane of '26, Miami Beach boasted its own power plant, a trolley, a pair of public schools, a church ("the best goddamn church there is," he promised, to appease his devout wife, Jane). Hollywood film crews descended now and then. Tourists followed the seasons. More than a couple dozen hotels were competing for bragging rights along the beaches, most following Fisher's lead. And despite the hurricane of '26, which all but erased the island (which Fisher rebuilt), and despite the implosion of real estate on the mainland, and despite even the Great Depression, Miami Beach kept growing: A little over six hundred people called it home the year the Flamingo opened; by 1930, almost 6,500 people did. And as the 1930s wore on elsewhere, they were marked, ironically, by growth in Miami Beach—all of it indebted to hotels, to the climate. Carpenters, bricklayers, plumbers, cooks, waiters, and coat-check girls all found work here. Fisher, meanwhile, went north to duplicate this fantastical blueprint in Montauk, Long Island, a project that barely got started before he declared bankruptcy in 1932.

The streak extended. The Second World War brought tens of thousands of enlisted soldiers into the hotels, falling into formation poolside, performing drills across the sands. After the war, the Art Deco dinosaurs on the island's south end began renting at seasonal rates. The streak crawled north, the splendor of the '20s morphing into the chintzy sensuality of the space age, with Morris Lapidus picking up the gauntlet Fisher had thrown down. Lapidus, an architect who'd cut his teeth designing department stores in Manhattan, took an evolutionary step with the Fontainebleau—five hundred and fifty rooms in a quarter-circle that hugged an Olympic ocean-side pool, a building praised for the bold elegance it projected but damned for the overkill of its interior, designed in a hybrid style the architect invented to please his client, known as "Modern French Provincial," or "Miami Beach French": oval columns, marble trimmed with gold (black marble, white marble, marble statuary, marble dummy fireplaces), wood antiques painted gold, a palette of two dozen colors smeared together, and a lobby staircase that seemed ripped from a Busby Berkeley set, snaking upward to an empty mezzanine. Lapidus raised, or bent, the bar with hotels like this one, up the beach, monstrously playful, so that by the end of the '60s, when the Republican Party arrived for its sun-blasted electoral convention, the Atlantic vista had been competing for some time with the glass-and-concrete circus that elbowed up to the edge of the water, what Norman Mailer likened to "piles of white refrigerator six and eight and twelve stories high, twenty stories high, shaped like sugar cubes and ice-cube trays on edge . . . buildings looking like giant op art and pop art paintings, and sweet wedding cakes, cottons of kitsch." This was Fisher's legacy, as translated by the Fontainebleau, a hotel that served as the measure for an amplified aesthetic, for the decade and the dozen or so hotels that followed, the Seville included.

My mother wasn't quite nineteen when she showed up at the Seville for her honeymoon. Until that day, she hadn't so much as left the house without a brother to chaperone her. Now a bride far from home, twelve hundred miles away from family, bound by God and the state of Pennsylvania to a man who was still mysterious to her, she was so wrecked by a case of nerves that she spent her first three days in Miami throwing up. (This nervous tick I inherited, spending two boyhood Christmas Eves in a row hospitalized from dehydration, the anticipation of Santa being too much, causing me to short-circuit—i.e., vomit—until the only recourse left was to stick an IV in my arm and deliver the truth: *Relax, son. There is no Santa Claus.*) So my mother and father darted about town, went to the beach, visited with relatives, ate paella at the Covadonga on Calle Ocho. But for the most part, she puked. "I was so sick and so happy," she told me. "Miami was a blur."

It took a few days, but she improved. Then, one evening, settling in after a day of sun, they received a phone call in their room from an officious-sounding gentleman. He invited them on a scenic tour of Central Florida, to see the alligators, smell the citrus, to behold the splendor of Indians and sugar. It sounded adventurous, a little educational. Best of all, it was free. All that was required of them was that they sit for a brief presentation at the end, a half-hour at most. They rose early the next morning and, as instructed, arrived in the lobby by daylight. They were greeted by a bus captain who escorted them, along with several other couples, all honeymooners, onto a Greyhound charter. Then they all headed for the swamp.

The tour was a gimmick, a trap, a means by which the Lehigh Acres Development Company lured potential buyers into the scrubby lowlands of Lee County, into a community not quite a town, but where, after five hours of driving through the swamp, with only a couple of stops and an orange-grove watchtower to break up the trip—and surprisingly few passengers throwing a fit after, say, the fourth hour—these sore and unsuspecting couples were led through a dazzling tour of model homes, then corralled into eight-by-eight offices to be worked over by hucksters peddling quarter-acre lots with the greasy hubris of Bible salesmen.

In hindsight, the bus ride alone seems like a borderline-criminal stunt. My mother thought it was painfully boring; my father seems rather sanguine about it. He remembers the bus captain blathering just to keep their attention. "He'd give a description of what we were driving through," Dad remembers, "like a description of the drainage canals—their history, what they do, what they accomplished. He'd get excited: 'Up ahead, we're going to pass through sugar cane fields!' And then he'd give you a dissertation on sugar cane. He talked about every little thing he could talk about on the way up there—the birds, the alligators, *everything.*"

My parents were sufficiently tenderized by the time they got to Lehigh Acres. The model homes were set on a roundabout known as Charmed Circle. Each model had a name—La Hoya, Raphael, Pelham, etc. The Whistler (2 bed/2 bath) and the El Greco (2 bed/1.5 bath) included screened porches. Each price promised a driveway, a cute etching in the sliding glass door, an oven, even a sidewalk superintendent. Folks could choose the option of a terrazzo floor, and even a built-in vacuum system. My parents swooned. "I remember these green, beaded curtains that separated the dining and living rooms," my mother told me. "The appliances, you had a choice of colors, avocado or harvest gold. I thought that was so exotic."

Across the street from Charmed Circle was a brand-new motel where actual buyers were invited to stay, free of charge, and celebrate their investment with a sangría at the Matador Room next door. Down the street from the motel was an A-frame church. The maps and brochures of future works promised a thriving community in full color—not too big, not too wealthy, but certainly white and by all means comfortable. My parents marveled at all of it there in the eight-by-eight room. A salesman, a young country boy, chatted with them about the virtues of raising a family in a solid community. Then he gave them some time to think about it. No pressure, just think about it. He went down the hall, discreetly repeating the script to other couples seated in their eight-by-eights. Then he came around again: What do you think?

It took about an hour, between stepping off the bus and being handed the ballpoint pen, for my parents to commit. Eight hundred and fifty dollars later, they owned a quarter-acre lot in Lehigh Acres, on the corner of Gene Avenue and Forty-eighth Street, right there on the canal that would someday, when each component of the grand vision was complete, carry them to their leisurely excursions on the Gulf. Land they would not set foot on or even see for forty years, but which seemed, at the time, not only a good investment, but a profoundly romantic gesture of faith in their future together. The next week, inspired, they dragged my mother's parents down to buy the lot next door.

L ee County—the interior of it, at any rate—was an improba-
ble spot for a paradise. Its legacy before World War II consisted of a handful of cattle ranchers who'd built small fortunes
on what brittle grass the cows could find. Spanish fisheries came
and went. Sawmills whined briefly, until the stretches of yellow
pine ran out, and once depleted the land was sold cut-rate to
start-up farmers who, in light of roads so treacherously dilapidated, shipped their goods to Fort Myers by way of the Caloosahatchee River—a miserably slow trip, creeping along, slow
enough that the crops often rotted en route. Making a living in
Lee County was a slog no matter how you looked at it.

But land was cheap. In 1951, Lee Ratner, a Chicago tycoon
who'd built tremendous wealth through mail-order, television,
and radio—hawking knives that cut through aluminum cans,
additives that boosted fuel efficiency, and even drink coasters—
sold a piece of his empire, a company that produced d-Con rat
poison, for a little over $10 million. Then he looked for a place
to hide his profits. Cattle ranches were a popular shelter for the

kind of wealth Ratner wanted to protect. He knew nothing about cattle, but that was the point: The losses would be tax-deductible. Ratner already owned a winter home in Miami Beach. He liked horses. Lee County was just a half-hour trip by plane, which Ratner also owned. For fifty bucks an acre, it all made sense. So, in 1951, he bought eighteen thousand acres, bought some horses, bought some cattle, and began spending incredibly expensive weekends on horseback in Lee County.

A young Miami advertising executive named Gerald Gould knew well who Ratner was, and knew that he wintered in Florida, and began to court him as a client. Ratner refused to abandon his Chicago agency, but he did agree to let Gould promote his next start-up, provided they came up with one. They spent the next several weeks brainstorming, on horseback, alighting, finally, on the idea of a cosmetics company. In the meantime, they formed a friendship, spending Saturdays on Ratner's land and flying back to Miami Beach in time to take the wives out for dinner—heavy tippers who knew all the bookies and managers at every hotel that had sprung up north of Lincoln Road, including the Fontainebleau, the Saxony, and another one of Gould's clients, the Seville.

Two years into the ranch, the tax provisions that let Ratner off the hook as a cattleman ran out. (Two years of losses in a row qualified as a "hobby" and thereby made the ranch taxable.) Ratner needed to either get rid of the land or make it profitable. He tried selling grasses—sod, alfalfa, bermuda—but that failed. Gould suggested he sell the land itself. Small lots for sale were already a leitmotif of the landscape, in road signs and billboards and in the paper. Success was common enough: A man with two or three hundred acres could divide it all up and sell ten to twenty lots a year, and make a decent living. Ratner would simply amplify the formula. His wealth had been built on a salesman's instincts, on days scouting the trade and country fairs and circuses where pitch men hawked his products, taking a handsome natural and putting him on camera, broadcasting the pitch, turning a thousand-dollar week into a hundred-thousand-dollar week. For Ratner, land would be just another product.

With the founding of Lee County Land & Title in 1954 (later named Lehigh Acres Development Corporation), Gould and Ratner began carving up the eighteen thousand acres of defunct cattle ranch into half-acre lots. They flew to New York to line up financing for the project. On the plane, with a barf bag flattened on the tray between them, they sketched out the hook: "You can own a full half acre in fabulous Florida! Only $10 down and $10 a month." Ratner's Chicago agency fleshed out the sketch, staged a photo with Ratner's niece sitting by a lake, took some shots of houses in towns nearby. They ran an ad in Northern papers, then produced a television infomercial based on the same idea—a pitch man, Ratner's niece, the lake, houses from other towns, an architect's rendering—and began pumping the mirage of Lehigh Acres across the country. Gould and Ratner sold over twelve thousand lots that first year, some for as little as five hundred dollars, with ten-dollar checks arriving by the sackful, poured onto the conference table at Gould's Miami office. And as the lots sold, they bought more land until, by the 1970s, Lehigh Acres covered over sixty thousand acres—150,000 lots, all told.

In the annals of real estate marketing, Lehigh Acres was an incredible success. In the history of urban planning, it was apocalyptic. The idea from the beginning—and exclusively—was to sell the lots, nothing more. No forethought was given to the possibility that someone might actually want to live there, no consideration given to streets or schools or sewers. The absurdity of the premise, that you could sell a worthless patch of land to people far away and expect them never to show up, was part of the logic of Florida real estate in the early 1950s, a logic that had evolved, so to speak, through technology. Mail order and television allowed the product to remain invisible, a product of the imagination. In the land boom of the 1920s, at least the suckers bothered to show up. Either way, by way of handshake or a coupon, the motive echoed between generations, guided by a Glengarry rule—*Get them to sign on the line that is dotted*. Selling, not building, was how these developers measured their success.

By 2009, Lehigh Acres made for a baffling cautionary tale. When President Obama landed in Fort Myers to announce his administration's response to the crisis, among the Lee County towns to choose from, he picked the town least blighted by the real estate implosion. Cape Coral and Fort Myers were hurting, but the effect of their foreclosures was remarkably different, since a good portion of them consisted of condominiums, a fallout neatly consolidated, neatly stacked, and largely hidden in the towers along the shore. Lehigh Acres's throes were much more severe, mainly because its fallout happened scattershot among duplexes and single-family homes that needed tending, and were left to crumble—all of it primed by an anarchy of building across parcels that had been sitting idle for years, and where developers finally sought to cash in, where more houses were built in the four years leading up to the president's visit than had been built in the previous fifty. On the day he delivered his speech, homes were selling for a third of what it had cost to build them.

In the summer of 2009, the *St. Petersburg Times* caught up

with Gerald Gould, in a feature that used Lehigh Acres as an omen of bad development, a story in which Gould owned up to the wreckage. "We gave so much thought to selling the land that the normal reservations for commercial properties, schools, all the ancillary things you need in a community, weren't made," he said. "We even had canals that ran uphill. I don't know any mistake you could make that we didn't make."

To be fair, the fallout of 2009 wasn't entirely Gould's and Ratner's doing. The basic provisions of a community—schools, parks, sewers, etc.—were added retroactively, zoned and mapped. But it was too late to consolidate all those long-distance land-owners into a town. Worse, since Lehigh Acres was never actually incorporated as a city, zoning over the decades was at the mercy of successive company presidents, so that hundreds of acres of commercial property were chopped up and sold to home developers at whim. Reflecting on all of it for the *Times*, Gould sounded both nostalgic and heartbroken, and even a little amazed by his and Ratner's naïveté. "We had no concept of people coming to live here," he told the *Times*. "That's the last thing we thought about."

That is, until the fall of 1955, when Gould got a call from a Wisconsin carpenter named Oran Gibbs, who'd bought land in Lehigh Acres after the first run of ads. For Gibbs, the time had come to retire, and with a brochure that listed several houses and prices, he called up Gould and ordered one, looking right at it—fourteen thousand dollars. He wanted it ready by spring.

Gould was flummoxed. There wasn't a single house anywhere in Lehigh Acres. There wasn't even a general store. There was only a fueling station for the road-construction and dredging crews. "Tell me something," he said. "When was the last time you were in Florida?"

"I've never been to Florida," Gibbs said.

"Don't you think you ought to come down and take a look at the place first?"

No, Gibbs was ready. The Milwaukee winters had worn him out. He wanted his house. He hung up the phone, mailed his check. Three months later, in the middle of February, he and his wife were spotted by a foreman, driving around in a U-Haul truck crammed with their possessions, looking to stake their claim, which they couldn't even find. Gould put their stuff in a warehouse, put them up in a Fort Myers motel, and had his crew slap a home together quick.

"That triggered the idea that we probably would have to be in the business of building houses," Gould said.

It sounded insane: that a town had grown *accidentally* out of some crackpot hybrid philosophy of *Always be closing* and *If you build it, pray they don't come*. And in one profile of Lehigh Acres after another, I never found a satisfying answer to the question of what they were thinking. The cautionary tale seemed over-simplified. A human remainder was missing, nagging at this implausible history. Lehigh Acres wasn't born simply out of chutzpah; there had to have been *some* kind of logic to it.

I spoke with Gould, who, at eighty-five, still lived in Miami. I asked him about his motive, if it was as brazen and reckless as it seemed in hindsight. How could he and Ratner have possibly expected to sell thousands of lots without expecting anyone to live on them? In a gentle, deadpan voice, a little dry with age, and thickened slightly by a Brooklyn accent that hadn't quite faded, he offered a bit of context, a peek into a long-dead way of thinking about real estate.

"It's not that we weren't concerned about whether or not

people would move there," he said. "But we found in taking surveys that a very, very small percentage of people that bought lots had any intention of building a house in the near term. These were young people in their thirties and forties, who thought they *might* build a house when they were sixty-five. But the idea was, that if they didn't buy the lot now, by the time they were sixty-five it was going to cost them so much more money that it *made sense* to buy it now."

Gould often followed up on those surveys, he said, by calling people who had sent in their ten bucks, just to color in the outline a little, to get to know his market. What he discovered in many cases, and to his and Ratner's advantage, was a tragic misunderstanding of how real estate actually worked—buyers who thought their land would grow tenfold in value in just a couple of years, or who thought their lot might actually be worth millions. He discovered people who didn't even know what, exactly, they had bought. "I interviewed one fella who said that the reason he bought the lot in Lehigh was because he had always dreamed of sitting on his back porch, and as far as his eye could see would be his land. A half acre."

He mentioned "the dream" over and over as we talked. It was his hook, but more complicated than the cliché I assumed he meant, a lifestyle one eventually realizes by picking up and moving to a new town, or into a new home. When he spoke of the dream, the dream was self-contained.

"Ninety percent of the people who bought the lots in Lehigh thought that *someday* they would be able to retire from hard work and move to wonderful Florida, have a beautiful home on a spacious lot, and enjoy their retirement forever. That was the dream. And people figured for ten bucks down and ten bucks a month, it was worth it, just to have that dream. And not only did they like to think about the *possibility* that they might retire here, they also thought, 'Wouldn't it be wonderful if we could tell our friends we owned property in Florida?' Even if they never had any intention of living on it. It was prestige owning a piece of land in Florida." The half- and quarter-acre parcels were as much intellectual property as anything else. Land in Lehigh Acres was bragging rights, which, in Gould's mind, was worth the ten dollars a month.

To clarify the mind-set of American consumer culture of the 1950s, Gould provided one more anecdote. "There was a fellow during those same years that advertised all over the United States in little classified ads—one-inch and two-inch classified ads: *This Is Your Last Chance to Send a Dollar to John Jones*. He didn't say he was selling them anything, he didn't say there was any reason to send it in. But he said, *This is your last chance to send a dollar!* That man was taking in a quarter of a million dollars a month"—an exaggerated success, surely, but even on a lesser scale befitting this circus history. "The Post Office finally stopped him," Gould said. "They couldn't put him in jail, 'cause he wasn't doing anything illegal, but they started to persecute him to make him stop, and he finally stopped. So the idea of ten-dollars-down-and-ten-dollars-a-month, this was revolutionary at the time. There were a lot of people who just sent it because they'd never heard of anything like that before. Then, of course, *everybody* started getting into it—remember Leonard Rosen, who developed Cape Coral, Golden Gate, Avon Park, on and on, he used to work in windows selling lanolin to make your hair beautiful and straighten out your hair and make it glow and this that and the other thing. That's the way he got his start. His brother, Jack, got his start selling crap on the boardwalk on Atlantic Beach. And that's the kind of mentality that got into the land business. Lee Ratner was sort of in that same class. The Mackle brothers. And we tried to keep it clean. But all of the companies that were big in the land business started off as promoters of one kind or another . . ." He realized he was beginning to ramble, paused, and brought it home.

"So if you want to know why people bought lots in Florida, they were *sold* lots in Florida."

The Seville Hotel was little more than a crumbling hulk, long shuttered, by the time I found it last summer. Its fate was typical: In 2005, the Ritz-Carlton Group partnered with another developer, Fortune International, to renovate the hotel and add a wing of condominiums to its east side, chasing yet another vision of a lifestyle utopia, part of the wave of conversions that led to stratospheric prices in Miami Beach real estate in the early 2000s. As the real estate market weakened, the Ritz-Carlton Group backed out, and by September 2009 the hotel's owners were facing foreclosure on the building. Now it was nothing more than a candy-colored tomb for those delusional expectations.

The day I was there, the only action at the hotel was at the bottom of the front steps: a couple of painters digging around inside a van, looking for tools for a job across the street; a handful of Haitian cab drivers leaning on their cars, chatting and smoking in the mid-afternoon sun. No one could tell me why the hotel had shut down, or what was planned for it. They couldn't even say how long it had been that way. An eight-foot chain-link fence blocked the lobby entrance. A few of the enormous tinted windows along the Collins Avenue façade had been shattered. On the ocean side of the building, the water sitting in the deep end of the pool had turned brown. I walked back out to the front and found a good spot to take a few pictures, kneeling on the grass roundabout that marked the site of the old Pancoast family hotel, one of the island's first. The giant clock on the Seville's façade was off by hours. A few clicks later, there wasn't much left to see. I got back in the truck, looped the roundabout, waved to the cabbies, then headed north on Collins Avenue to follow the route that the bus had taken on its way to Lehigh Acres, long ago.

N.W. Thirty-sixth Street is crowded, but doesn't offer much in the way of sightseeing, and offered less in 1969. The street runs past dilapidated shopping centers—a Marshall's, a Target, an empty space where a big-box merchant once anchored the strip. It cuts through the Design District, then through a clutter of Burger Kings and hardware shops and gas stations and used-car lots, past door manufacturers and body shops and a church. Now and then I'd see one of a dozen motels—The Fantasy Inn, the Chesapeake, the Crossway, the Hialeah Executive—whose chintzy flair betrayed its age. I drove, and drove, taking the street until it merged with Route 27, through Miami Springs and Okeechobee Road, past Hialeah. I spotted the canal that ran alongside the road, the one my father remembered from the '69 tour. The street dipped under an overpass for Flagler's old railroad, then continued through a stretch of more motels, as anonymous as government buildings, and even one motel with palm trees on its sign, the sign itself flanked by real palms, the simulacrum resonating with dumb redundancy. Mini storage units seemed like a thriving business in these parts.

Once across the Palmetto Expressway, the buildings receded, the vista opened up, and blank plots of grass and sand replaced the commercial footholds. At a trailer park, a handmade sign— *SOLDADURA*—advertised some fellow's skill in soldering. Two-story terracotta condos marked where the road widened to six lanes, where the grass median thickened, and where signs advertising LAND FOR SALE began to appear. I flew past a landscaping van with the message *JESUS CRISTO SALVA* painted on the side, larger than the name of the business itself. There was a Home Depot on the horizon. Then Hialeah Gardens, where on satellite maps the bright red roofs attest to how new the homes are, and how closely set, like bright vertebrae coiled and looped, no backyards to speak of, just a pair of boxes backended together and repeated by the thousands. Past another condo development, a brown-and-pink scheme. Past 118th Avenue and Rancho Gaspar, Rancho Grande, and a tight, tall grove of blurry Australian pine shooting up in the middle of a wide stretch, where the highway turned a blinding white and blended with the milk-colored haze of the sky. And farther along, on the shoulder of the highway, signs for pony rides and palm-tree nurseries. White, spindly, leafless melaleuca. A crematorium like some bureaucratic headquarters from Brasilia dumped in the middle of the marsh. And then nothing but sugar cane and the hardscrabble morass settlers and laborers and prisoners hacked at for three centuries, and mostly tamed, a feat their heirs have come to regret. In the distance, to the west, a cement plant chugged a white plume into the white sky.

An hour or so later, you come to Lake Okeechobee, and know it not by the glittering water, but by the fifty-foot berm that traps it, an alien hillside to the sawgrass and marsh. Route 27 hugs it, bending east. My father climbed this berm when he was younger, just to see what was on the other side. I, too, was curious, and so I yanked a hard right onto a shell path that led me to the top, to a dam lock. I parked, got out, took a few steps, and stared out across a dishwater vista. I took a few snapshots with the plastic camera. A pair of old men were fishing near the lock and had gotten their lines tangled. The haze was strong by now. The scene was just short of ugly. The pond-apple swath described with reverence in settlers' journals was long gone, sucked dry for the benefit of the farms envisioned by the champions of reclamation, farms that I passed on the way up. Score: 1 for the Vision.

But only by standing here and taking in the view, on both sides of the levee, does one begin to comprehend that epic task and its consequences, the irreparable ecological damage of putting those farms in place. Only by driving through the swamp (along the Tamiami Trail, say), and certainly by walking *into* it does one begin to comprehend the arsenal of machines and dynamite and body count it took to tame this place. And only by standing here does one get a good visceral sense of the impact of all that science and ambition. Taming the billions of gallons that seeped from this lake southward to the sea was the first order of business in ushering Florida into the modern era, so that it could catch up with the rest of civilization. Seven hundred square miles of water nine feet deep, a vast puddle that spilled slowly toward the Straits, forming what Marjory Stoneman Douglas christened the "River of Grass." The state had a hell of a time getting all that water to behave. Hamilton Disston's populist vision of farmers making their living off small crops in the muck never quite took shape. Hurricanes simply scooped those farmers away; floods arrived with an erasing power. And with each catastrophe, the Corps of Engineers simply revisited the dike to build it higher, until finally, after the farmers had given up, and the era of agro-industrial farming was in full swing, the lake was no longer a threat. Of course, a reckoning awaits for making so much water behave so unnaturally, but that's the price you pay for an Eden of lettuce.

———

NOT a mile inside Lee County, with Lake Okeechobee about an hour behind me, through scents of citrus and horseshit, past earth-movers dredging along the shoulder of the road, I saw the first sign of real estate trouble, on the north side of 80, where the landscape shifted from orange groves to a stretch of torqued, spindly scrub oak blackened from a fire, a charred treeline running a quarter mile or so before a gap opened and the white-washed gates of Caloosa Preserve appeared, clean but with no signs of life, and only one roof peeping above the burned trees. I turned around and drove back, rolled up to the gate. The guard-house was finished, spotless inside (at least from what I could see through the glass), and empty.

A trim, paved road, not a piece of trash anywhere, and the blackened oak stretched in all directions, with a thick understory of palmettos hugging those tall black threads. I approached a small landscaped median planted with a yellow sign, its slithering arrow reminding me to pass on the right side, as if it mattered now. I went left. On the next median rose a magnificent live oak, untouched, followed by a median with another sign, the medians alternating this way for a while. Slim, fake-brick pallets marked the addresses of houses that were never built. The intentions and emptiness blended together, creepy at first, like driving through some prehistoric diorama. I waited for *something* to pop out of the brush—a mechanical Tyrannosaurus, a goon dragging a body. However sinister or fantastical, it would have fit.

Finally, after twisting through roundabouts, the blackened trees fell away to reveal tall grass and groves of palms and oaks, a savanna marked on the far side by a thicker line of trees. As I took a bend around a lake, I could see a house—two stories, a Spanish-tile roof, with its own landscaped roundabout in the driveway. For sale, of course, with the builder's sign in the front yard. Vultures hunkered on the roof. I pulled into the driveway, got out, clapped. A vulture unfolded its wings, stretched wide, then whipped off. I approached the front steps, stepping over feathers on the brick, and peeked through the enormous glass pane of the front door, past an immaculate emptiness—the tile floor bright, the fireplace finished, the interior a weird conflu-ence of Mediterranean and colonial touches—straight back to the sliding glass doors and onto the patio and pool. The water looked brackish. There was something electric about this house's abandonment, something archaeologically pure. And then, as if on cue, a vulture waddled into the frame, turned its neck, and stared at me. I wanted to shoot it.

How many of those fuckers were back there? I went around the side of the house to see, singing and barking and whistling and, as I approached an iron fence that marked the edge of the pool, taking slower steps. A pair of vultures were perched on the rail, and flew away as I got closer. And then, clearing the corner, I saw, like some nightmare variation of that cinematic moment when a secret door is opened and the soldiers of the under-ground resistance are revealed (leaning over maps, cleaning weapons, tweaking the short-wave), about a dozen vultures that all twitched at once. They stretched their necks and puffed up and leveled their stares, spread themselves wide open. A couple went airborne. I turned and left.

Driving again, I reached a cul-de-sac and slowed, awestruck

by a wall of blond guinea grass that reached well above six feet. At the edge of the cul-de-sac, a white permit box was nailed to a post, marking the beginning of a path that cut through the grass toward the river. I threw the gearshift to park, left the radio on and the car running, got out and walked toward the field. The permit box was empty, just a home to wasps now. I looked down the path and could see, far away, a dock that stretched out over the Caloosahatchee, the big perk of the neighborhood.

Walking down the path, pushing the grass away, I could hear the wind brush the field, and could just make out the fading chatter on the car radio. A fraud trial had begun that day, in which a pair of Bear Stearns managers were accused of conspiring to hide the frailty of hedge funds based on subprime mortgages, investments prosecutors contended the managers knew were "at risk of collapse." It was the first criminal case to emerge from the crisis. Lawyers and brokers were paying close attention, since it would set the tone for future trials. More importantly, the case had become a lightning rod for an angry public seeking a target, an anger seeded in the bailout of Wall Street, and exacerbated by the disparity between the fates of brokers and everyone else. In a month's time, and after just a six-hour deliberation, the jury would acquit the accused, contending that bad investing and criminal intent weren't the same thing. Of course, the verdict hardly satisfied their peers in the general public. And considering all the wealth that had evaporated in the hands of such well-paid professionals, it was easy to understand the idea that the loss of so much savings should be punished.

And yet, walking down the path, the river glittering ahead, I didn't sense a tragedy. I certainly couldn't sympathize for developers here, not after scaling it next to the deacon's losses, or, whatever their mistakes, the Trodys', or of any of the families I'd seen displaced. Visions of Italianate mansions had failed to materialize on these lots, but it was a disappointment that paled next to a life on the street. The upshot was that Caloosa Preserve was, in its suspended state, a kind of paradise. One simply had to reassess the emptiness, consider this natural blank slate a virtue, and see the sublimity in a dock with no house attached. The placid waters, the quiet flutter of the palms: This subdivision had accidentally lived up to its name, reverting, in essence, to the preserve its developers had aspired to pretend. Things would pick up soon enough, and the clacking of hammers would fill the air again. It would be a welcome sound for good reason, but certainly the end of whatever wild was left along this path to the river.

Passing the lake again, I noticed a turtle on its shell in the middle of the empty street. What had flipped it? A buzzard, maybe, trying to lift off with the thing. Vultures flew in a vortex high overhead, waiting. The natural order was slowly falling back into its groove. Was it foolish to think the neighborhood would be better off in the hands of the state? A gift to the parks system? All around me, a new reclamation was avenging the reclamation that preceded it. And while romanticizing the failure of this development might have seemed naïve, it seemed no less foolish to regard the interrupted subdivision—the ghost subdivision—as a tragic symbol of the crisis. For a year or so, the images of ghost subdivisions were broadcast and printed as cautionary portraits, aimed at triggering a kind of lamentation, as if the American Dream had slipped away. Suddenly, the suburb was sorely missed. The sentiment seemed a bit shortsighted. In boom times, for my generation, at least, we loathed the subdivision. We labeled it a homogenizing, unimaginative place. So it was curious, during the crisis, to be asked to pity its condition. Too many empty houses can be depressing, sure, but I never got the sense that the couple who had chosen to live away from the city, and who planned on staying in their home awhile, minded the extra space.

So the ghost subdivision had become the symbol of—what, exactly? Of having fewer neighbors? Of living next to unkempt grass? The ghost subdivisions I drove through, like this one, seemed peaceful. Awkward, yes, pocked with junk here and there, but mostly peaceful, a far cry from inner-city neighborhoods where foreclosures served as the long-awaited excuse to raze a block. What's more, as I drove through one ghost subdivision after another, I spotted kids hard at play. I suppose seeing them was nostalgic, too, a throwback to my own childhood in North Carolina, where, along the edge of my neighborhood, where the streets dead-ended into pastures, or crumbled into the pines, where the man-made stuff hesitated, things took on a theatrical aspect. All along this perimeter were the gloomy corners we visited on bikes, firing bottlerockets from our handlebars into the trees, where we descended upon the farthest cul-de-sacs littered with spent firecrackers, beer cans, panties, condoms—doleful clues to the dark fun of adults. This trash made us nervous, but it was the stuff of life nonetheless. So the boys jumping on an abandoned sofa among the weeds of a ghost subdivision were probably getting a taste of the weird country life of other children, far away, and likely much poorer. Those mattresses and broken sofas weren't that much of a stretch from my own Carolina expeditions. Sad circumstances, certainly, but I took comfort in seeing those kids build something out of all that crap, a planet of their own, making that ghost subdivision come alive.

Heading west, the scenery toughened up. The houses were smaller, the landscape more hardscrabble. I was on a two-lane blacktop that narrowed into the horizon, coursing straight through a smattering of block homes—some finished, some not—that popped into view between stretches of cypress and pine. Side streets shot off into the cypress marsh. Every half mile or so, I'd turn to see where one led and drive through woods until the road ended at a weedy cul-de-sac or until the pavement simply crumbled apart, as if the road crew had given up, with street signs sticking out of the dirt. When houses did appear, they did so in clusters, like huts tucked off the path, a few with roofs missing (unfinished or scavenged, it was difficult to tell). These neighborhoods had a disposable vibe to them, but a gloomy pioneering thrill, too, something brave about the neighbors who, after clawing out a spot, were holding fast. A minivan's backseat served as a porch bench in front of one home; between others, in a flooded ditch that separated a row of small backyards, a tricycle lay tipped over, just a dozen feet from the neighbor's garbage

can drowning in the same ditch—backyard surrender all down
the line.

Near Richmond and Jasmine Roads, things normalized a bit.
The blocks filled out, the yards looked tended, save for an overgrown lawn here and there. Every now and then I could see
Code Enforcement's yellow notice taped to a door. Overall the
scene looked more like Clearwater than a ground zero. At a stop-
light, I slowed and waited, and watched a crossing guard with
her piping whistle shepherd children across the street. I watched
the traffic's slight bustle. The scene was busy but not too hectic,
an all-American normalcy.

I pulled into a modest, cream-colored office complex and
parked. Before setting out from Miami, I'd tracked down a man
named Rick Anglickis, who was working for Gould and Ratner
around the time my parents showed up. He was, as luck would
have it, part of the stable of salesmen who worked those honeymooners over in the eight-by-eight rooms. Anglickis had agreed
to talk and show me around. Inside the building, I walked down
a cream-colored hallway, as bland as the cream outside, deco-
rated a good twenty years ago. I found his office: the Heritage
Group, a real estate company that handled just about every aspect
of the business—investment, development, consulting, on and
on, with a very American eagle (arrows in one claw, olive branch
in the other) stamped on the signage. The front desk was abandoned. I called out, and Anglickis emerged from a conference
room. He was tall and barrel-chested, a blond paling with age.
He wore a floral-patterned shirt, pressed shorts, loafers, and had
an accent that blended the ensemble together—a hammy Chicago *bah*, like a fat man sitting on his vowels.

Anglickis, now middle-aged, still lived in Lehigh Acres, and
had become one of the community's most intense champions, a

godfather of sorts—former president of the local Jaycees, builder, salesman, with his hand in, and name on, hospitals, parks, community centers, and the like. Just a transplant forty years ago, he'd become a loyal citizen.

We passed a gold shovel leaning in a corner, a gift from the local recreation center for his help in building it. He led me back into the conference room, where I sat opposite an enormous color-coded map of Lehigh Acres, the same one Gould and Ratner used long ago, showing all of Ratner's sixty thousand acres and then some.

I asked him to show me my family's quarter-acre in relation to the rest of the town. He stood and waved across the purple center of the map, the zone that represented the heart of the community, where we were. "This here is about fifty percent of the population of Lehigh Acres," he said. "This is pretty much about where the city water-and-sewer system exists. There's a small run of sewer and water that goes up this way, and a little bit down here. But basically this is it." He glanced down at the sheet of paper in his other hand, peeking over his glasses. "Your property is out in . . . section thirteen . . ." His hand slid northeast, and kept going, toward a brown zone, well away from the purple center. "You're where there is no water and no sewer." He looked at me. "And not even in your children's children's children's children's lifetime—and I've told you the first lie because I didn't put enough children in there—will there be water and sewer out there. Because it costs an incredible amount of dollars to put in one foot of water and sewer. And until they can hook up people to the water and sewer lines, it just doesn't pay." In other words, until the empty lots filled with homeowners, there would be no tax base to cover the cost of installing the infrastructure; but in order to attract homeowners in the first place, a water and sewer system needed to exist. It was a public works catch-22 rooted in the sales pitch fifty years ago.

When the trend shifted in the late 1950s, when people began building on the land they'd bought, Gould and Ratner scrambled to form a utilities company to provide all the amenities of a normal town—water, sewer, power—but, since it was an incredibly expensive retroactive plan, only for a small portion of those 150,000 lots. To avoid the infrastructure conundrum Anglickis was pointing out, Gould offered to swap lots with the buyers who were farthest from the infrastructure for lots closer to it. Some accepted, others passed. It was, after all, their right to choose. Either way, the plan was scrapped after Gould left the company. Now it was being resurrected by county commissioners, under a new rubric, the Lehigh Plan, though it was slow going. So many years of building had spread like a brush fire. The result was that in order to repair Lehigh Acres, an unlikely level of cooperation was required, from developers and contractors and homeowners alike. "The difficulty over the years has been assembling property so that it can be used intelligently," Anglickis said. "But unless you get a block of lots all at once, you can't do much. So no matter what they come to you for—park, school, road—unless it's something they can take you to court and say you *must* sell it at a reasonable price, the development is held up by the individual property owners. And all it takes is a couple of lots to hold back." The installment-plan dream had backfired.

Anglickis was, of course, speaking as an advocate of a growth much smarter than the one he'd promoted forty years ago, which he admitted. "Back then," he said, "the object of the game was to cut the lots up into little pieces and to sell them for ten dollars down and ten dollars a month to as many people as we could."

To do that, they launched an advertising campaign that took

on the aspects of a traveling circus. "We'd set up a model home in a snow-filled parking lot," he said, sweeping his hand wide, "with orange smudge pots around the home, and chicks in bikinis laying out underneath palm trees and an elephant walking around with a big flap that said FLY TO FLORIDA FOR PEANUTS. We'd load people up on Super G Constellations—a hundred and five seats at a time, piling those people in there—and we'd fly them down to Fort Myers, meet them with a bus, pile them into the bus, take them on the same trip your parents took. That was the business. That's what we did."

If it was all a hustle, I wondered if he thought the cautionary tale was fair. The *Times* story still irked him. "I could show them more sales today than in any period in the history of our community," he said. "I could show them where a bank foreclosed on a house and it was sold to another family, and the house was pretty and the family was delighted. But is *that* the story they choose to run? No. Instead, they find Gould, who loves this community more than anything on the planet, and he says, 'Yeah, in retrospect, I guess we did some things wrong.' And *that* became their headline. I can tell you that in 1950, when Gould and Ratner were developing Lehigh Acres, it was *way* beyond its time. They did things that were unheard of in development. Fifty years later, looking back—well, gosh, I guess we shouldn't have sold those lots to those people one at a time. We thought Fort Myers was going to be the commercial town, and that we were going to be the bedroom community. We didn't plan a whole lot of commercial stuff—we didn't need to. So I guess when you look back after fifty years, you know . . . but if you talk to people in this town, the longer someone has resided in this community, whether they're thirty or ninety, you'll find that they all have this burning desire to express that this is the greatest place on earth. But are those the interviews they ran in the paper? No. We went on a tour, we passed some houses that were overgrown with weeds and broken out, and *those* were the pictures they took, and *that* was the story they ran, so that everything about this community sucks. The *media*."

Charmed Circle was on the sightseeing list, though I needed Anglickis to help me find it. "It's gone now," he said, clearly dispirited. "The motel's gone, the restaurant's gone. They knocked it all down." The building that housed the sales offices was still intact, though, and included one of his favorite haunts, a diner called Rosie's, open breakfast and lunch only. We headed there along Leeland Heights Boulevard, cutting through different neighborhoods. Some looked clean, stable, healthy; in others there were frazzled yards with tilted FOR SALE signs, more Code Enforcement notices taped to long-abandoned doors, shadows of the next wave. Anglickis insisted there was an economic uptick under way, which he could prove through the success of his own business. What bugged him was the media's cynicism, its insistence on ignoring the town's various signs of health. In his mind, this last fallout was just part of the cycle. "It only feels different because you're not remembering the last one," he said, "or the one before that, or the one before that. I can tell you that the last one, in the '80s, interest rates were at eighteen percent. So things were really ugly the last time. Eighteen percent and people were still buying. They're buying today. The market is terrific. It really is. But if the media keeps telling everybody we're in the tank, I guess people start to believe we're in the tank."

We pulled into the parking lot of a low, coral-colored building, where Rosie's and a pilates studio were apparently the only tenants. "This is where you went to buy," Anglickis said. He pointed to a field of weeds and wild flowers, a couple of palms, a few piles of sand. "Across the street, where all that waste is, is Charmed Circle." I looked at the golf course just ahead. The putting green was overgrown, shoddy, swallowed.

We got out, crossed the parking lot, and entered Rosie's through a glass door—the only natural light in the room, the only view. Anglickis waved to a few friends finishing up their lunch, then found a table. The waitress came by, they chatted. She scribbled down our orders—a burger and an Arnold Palmer for Anglickis, the chicken tenders for me—and darted off promising cornbread in a minute. On the way out the door, the small bell chiming, two cops teased him warmly and waved.

I tried to glance around and get a sense of those eight-by-eight rooms. I shouldn't bother, Anglickis said, the place had been totally reconfigured. But this was it, the neurological center of what he called "the trap."

I asked him about the ruse that brought my parents up from Miami.

"We had probably fifty hotels we worked with in Miami Beach," he said. "We did a lot of vacation certificates—four days, three nights—and we booked people into resorts in Miami Beach or Fort Lauderdale, St. Pete, Clearwater. The vacation certificate required you to sit in a land-sales presentation. We called them 'hooker certificates,' cause we hooked you into the presentation. Then there was a group of solicitors whose job it was to contact people who happened to be staying at a hotel or beach, who got paid for every unit—or a buying couple—they would book into a hospitality room or bus trip or plane ride. That's where your folks came in. They got on a bus. Some people were vacation certificate holders down for their free vacation, some were random to fill up the rest of the bus. The best buyers we tried to put on a plane, because that would get them to the salesman in Lehigh first, before they got worn out. Those were the couples we thought were the best units. The second-best units were put on the bus. Those we couldn't get, one or two we'd put into hospitality rooms. These people would all come to Lehigh and go on a tour and then go into the closing rooms. We might send some of them out with a private chauffeur and a car to look at the land, but more often they were looking at something they were told was their lot, and nowhere close to where their lot actually was."

I mentioned a detail my father shared, of the salesman working several rooms at once. "Actually," Anglickis said, "every office was bugged. What they did was, they'd go back to the sales manager's office and hear what you were talking about, what your objections might be. Now the salesman is a lot smarter, and he comes back. There was also a turnover salesman, whose job was to revive what appeared to be a dead sale. And he'd revive it through a sales pitch, baloney. He was always sitting at the bugging station, listening to several conversations, and if he heard a sale was getting away, he'd walk in and say, 'Jeez, I got some good news, hate to interrupt you guys, but you remember that corner lot right next to the canal that was sold yesterday? Well, the deal fell through. I just wanted you to know that it's back on the market. The other buyers already put a thousand down, and the boss just told me he'll sell it for the difference.' Funny stuff."

The cornbread arrived. "The salesman would leave the room," he said, "and from the bugging station we could hear whoever it was in there. They'd say to each other, 'We just need to think about this. We need to pray over it tonight.' So the salesman would come back in and he would say, 'Now listen, I don't want to force you people into doing something that you'll be hasty about. And I hope you don't think I'm too corny, but I've always found that when I'm ready to make a big decision, my wife and I, we always go to the Lord and ask for some wisdom. So if you don't mind right now . . ." he began wheezing, a belly laugh. He put his cornbread down. "We used to just *die*. You know, the next day, they're *signing* hard and *pushing* hard and all excited. I used to love it when a salesman got the 'We gotta think about it and pray over this' thing. They would buzz me and say, 'We got one!' And I'd come across the street just to hear them pray.

"It became such a factory. The salesmen didn't even fill out the contracts. They'd go back to the central office, the girls would fill out the contracts, give it back to the salesman, and he'd go get the signatures. And the button-up guy would come in, give the gifts to the customers. The buyers were invited to the Matador Room for sangría. The non-buyers went to the motel. They weren't treated poorly, mind you, they just didn't get sangría."

Talking about his fellow salesmen was obviously nostalgic for him. He admired their styles, their schticks. I reached down and dug through my satchel for a folder full of paperwork my father had kept over the years, and found the sales contract for the lot. My parents couldn't recall much about the salesman they'd met that day, but when I showed Anglickis the contract, he smiled. "Mark Bateman," he said. "He was with us for twenty-five years. He lives over in Alva." Bateman's was a Southern schtick, Anglickis said. "He was the Southern gentleman the wife would fall in love with, because of the way he talked. He was a young, good-looking guy. He grew up here, so he'd talk about the experiences he benefited from in a town like this. And of course he's shooting at this being a great place to live, raise a family, all that."

Most of those guys had come and gone. Artie went to Orlando, opened a time-share, sold it for millions. Bobby, whom Anglickis hired as a bus captain in Miami, was now a VP of sales and marketing in Tampa. One guy still worked out of his garage, selling lots for fifty down and fifty dollars a month. Mark was over in Alva doing who knows what. Anglickis remembered them wistfully, and with pride. These were, it seemed, a salesman's glory days.

Was there an irony in Anglickis sticking around—and not just living in Lehigh Acres, but being so passionate about it? For him it wasn't so much an irony as a slow road to Damascus. They sold the hell out of this place, he insisted, because selling both made them lots of money and eventually led to growth. It was as if they had tasted the Kool-Aid, knew what was in the Kool-Aid, and wanted everyone else to have a glass, too. "Everything before I came was geared toward retirement—that word was in every piece of literature. The real sense of building a community began once Charmed Circle was built. Everybody bought into building the community. That's the thing that drove everybody. We *expected* to sell a hundred homes in June, we *expected* to sell a million dollars' worth of land a month. Because we were going to be a city, and it was going to have three hundred thousand people someday. We even started to plan the land differently. We added curvilinear streets, just to break the monotony of what had been designed before, because that would make it a better place to live. The underlying drive was always to build a city. And I can tell you honestly, that's what's kept me."

"You mean you actually bought into something you never thought was going to happen?"

He sipped his drink. "I'm actually writing a book," he said. *"The Lies We Told That Came True.* I'll fill a lot of chapters. And sure, the guys that moved on all built a second life in some other city. But my friends were here. I started the little league, and Babe Ruth baseball, and Cub Scouts and, you know, I was building the city. Got on the company that built the hospital. I could drive you by the athletic complex that has my name on it, at a high school, our first high school. It's a part of the community, it's a part of my fabric. To go somewhere else and make eight million dollars a year is of no interest to me."

And through one monologue after another of his fierce boosterism, Anglickis broke down the ecology of what he loved about this business, the interplay between predator and prey that made real estate a wondrous ecosystem. The suckers weren't just suckers, but incremental to the evolution of the town that over forty years he had grown to love, and build, and lead. "The reason this community has grown is because of people like your parents. They bought this piece of useless garbage 'cause they were shlucked off a beach somewhere, enjoying their vacation, dragged across Florida, put into a little tiny office half this size, beat on until they bought, and then they sent their ten dollars for ten years to some wasteland across the way. Never came down, never had an idea. But the other guy in the office next to them spent his lifetime *dreaming* about coming to his lot in Lehigh Acres when he retired. So for fifty years guys have been paying off their lots, and they come down to Lehigh Acres, and some of them say, 'Holy crap, what a piece of junk this place is! I'm going to go to Tampa!' And the next guy says, 'I've been waiting for this all my life.' And so for fifty years there's been this steady flow, the economy be damned. Now, some people paid for their lots, were going to sell them to the next guy, and found out there was no next guy. Some folks sold their lots for forty thousand and made a deal. And over the years, those things have spiraled and changed. Maybe your lot won't be forty thousand again, maybe it will. But overall, in the long run, it'll cycle up and it'll cycle up, and it'll cycle up."

Meanwhile, the cycle's length remained a mystery.

———

AFTER dropping Anglickis off at his office, I went looking for my parents' lot, driving through patches of the all-American, middle-class experience Gould and Ratner had promised, what Anglickis and his fellow salesmen had hawked. I followed the directions he'd left me to his own neighborhood, where his company built several dozen homes to compete with the styles Gould and Ratner offered. It was one of the most charming neighborhoods I'd seen in a while—not wealthy, nor crushed under the weight of mansions, but clean, with a wide street, and single-story, block-and-stucco homes, each a cousin to the ranch style, white and off-white and sometimes very white, all low as if to duck the heat, every mailbox straight. More importantly, they were all on level ground, with gutters, not a well or septic mound in sight.

But the scenery snapped to fallout with as little as a left turn. Here the houses wrestled with the creeping mass of vines and brush of the empty quarter-acre lots that surrounded them on either side. Some houses were veiled in bushes. The architecture was lazier than in the center of town: one-story cookie-cutters with thick portico columns and white Romanesque windows. Some houses stood half-finished, roofless, with rebar poking through the cinderblock like a thousand compound fractures rusting in the sun. Other homes looked prepared for the worst, shuttered with plywood and metal—sheets bolted to the windows and drilled over the door.

In a part of town called "Little Baghdad," I saw what Anglickis claimed was the heart of the town's bleak statistics. Here was an entire community of duplexes, hundreds of acres of houses built to flip and rent cheap, where pride of ownership was never intended as part of the equation. These were, in essence, houses built with the same commitment and care as if they'd come with a returnable receipt, where at the housing bubble's peak the asking prices reached as high as $200,000, and where they were now worth about $60,000 at best. Duplexes with screened-in front patios that were barely three feet deep; with shell-and-sand front yards; duplexes shaped like horseshoes, with two garages flanking the ends, and a pair of small windows in the shallow belly in between. Considering the portion of each duplex dedicated to the garage, I began to wonder if the developers intended it less as a perk to protect a tenant's car than as more square footage to help them split the rent.

Driving along Forty-eighth Street, where the shell and gravel road turned to pavement for a while, I found Gene Avenue, the corner that marked my parents' lot. But I would have passed it if not for a sweet, strange vision: Across the street, guarded by a pair of enormous bright-green *agave* cactus, behind a chainlink fence that lined an acre as thick and varied as a royal garden, stood a beach house, vinyl-sided, raised high on wood stilts to clear the coastal floods, which were irrelevant this far inland, so that really what those stilts afforded was an unimpeded view of the fallout that surrounded the sanctuary these owners had cultivated. The front yard was a frenzy of landscaping, full of whimsical touches. Cactus shouldered up to palms and conifers. Plastic flamingoes hid in a thicket. Clay frogs hunkered underneath an evergreen. A pair of clay rabbits guarded the gravel driveway. The fence itself was draped with birthday party stars on twine woven in between the links. In one corner, next to a slouching Royal palm, an American flag whipped on a pole. Every festive detail of this house was an antidote to everything around it.

I pulled up to one of the *agaves*, shut the truck off, and crossed the street to my parents' lot, which sat about another thirty yards down a narrow road. I high-stepped over the weeds and grass that pushed up through the asphalt, dodged the thorny second-growth, then waded into waist-high grass until I reached the canal. The brush rustled: small, startled creatures. I'd disturbed whatever peace had fallen over this place.

When my parents bought this property, the literature they took with them promised a bright future, with plenty of options, a "52 week a year vacation" in a home that offered "all the privacy and convenience you want plus a way of life where upkeep and responsibility give way to full-time fun." Included in their collection is a map from 1982, published by an investment company, that lists Lee County as a place of great potential, with its population expected to grow by over eighty thousand residents in ten years' time. The map's four-color Florida is surrounded by rockets and waterskiers, sailboats and sunfish, cargo tankers and newlyweds on a stroll, splendid bridges, and goofy swamp rats. Curiously, on the brochure they took with them the day they bought the lot, the cover is a bird's-eye view of Lehigh Acres, a panoramic shot of hundreds of homes, without a single breathing soul on the streets, nor a single car. My father kept every brochure from that visit in 1969, and over the years kept every letter, every postcard, every piece of paper sent to him by some agent or entity asking to buy it, offering cash on the spot. Postcards, contracts, three-page letters with business cards stapled to the corner, and picture after picture of agents who persisted, aging slightly over the span of letters, but always wearing that same prom-night smile.

These letters tell the story. In 1997, my father couldn't have gotten more than $2,000 for this lot. Seven years later, the asking price had crept up to just $9,000, shooting up to $13,000 before the year was out. Then, in 2005, the bubble's skin began to stretch. Postcards began offering him $23,000 and a little more, and the price kept climbing. He got letters from realtors, schoolteachers (or realtors posing as schoolteachers), from a retired couple (or a realtor posing as a retired couple). Letters from investors advising him that "now is the best time to CA$H IN your long term investment." Letters alerting him that lots nearby were selling for $46,000 and $55,000. My father's pencil marks are still on one letter, sent from an agent named "Marty"—faint circles around a sum, with light strokes underlining Marty's promises and predictions, and spindly arithmetic sketched in the letter's margins, a delicate calculation, barely touching the paper, as if whispering to himself through the pencil while Marty rattled on. The offers sweetened. One company, Douglas Realty, offered him $25,000 in January 2005, then $35,000 just three months later. Finally, in June 2005, the Palm Real Estate Group wrote to him with a promise of $40,000 for the lot. None of it seemed real to him. He was convinced it was all some kind of scam. But it was the peak of a now vanished fortune. The offers were real, and, more absurdly, represented only 80 percent of what the brokers would get once they sold the land to developers looking to buy lots by the dozen.

Forty thousand dollars for a sandbox. I stood there looking at the brush, picking burrs off my pants. A hot wind picked up. I couldn't imagine this land being worth a tenth of what those hucksters had promised. This land would never be worth that much again, certainly not in my father's lifetime, probably not in my own. Or, thinking optimistically, I might see it as a doddering octogenarian, after I'd moved to Lehigh Acres and built a miniature version of our Carolina home to retire in, spending my mornings looking for signs of life in that brackish ditch, waiting for a neighbor or candy-striper to pick me up, to take me to the Walgreen's on the corner so I can fill a prescription—or, better, being stubborn enough and nimble enough to drive there myself.

I walked back to the truck. I looked up at the house on stilts, and could see a man and woman standing there on the second-story deck, watching me. They descended the tall, rickety steps of the deck, crossed onto the lawn, then disappeared behind the tight cluster of trees before reappearing on opposite sides of a conifer. They walked up to the fence and leaned on it. The man was slight, about five-foot-six, his clothes loose, as if he'd thinned-out unexpectedly. His long face was masked in black sunglasses and a floppy booney hat.

He nodded. "What's going on, brother."

I pointed back at the lot. "That's my inheritance," I said.

He leaned and looked over my shoulder. "Yeah, well, what are you gonna do with it?"

"I don't know. What do you think I should do with it?"

He grinned. "I mean, prices are fucked up," he said, then he shook his head. "I don't know."

His name was Wink Parent. He had a slow, deep, cracker drawl. His wife, Sarah, waved. Her long hair, wheat and gray, had been wrestled into a thick braid, with bangs she wiped away as the wind tossed them. She wore a squinting smile when she talked.

I asked them about the house. It was indeed a beach house,

Wink said, which they'd found abandoned on Sanibel Island. They were living in Fort Myers at the time, and had decided to leave the city for something a little more quiet, and, after Hurricane Bob, a little farther inland. The lot was cheap, the house was cheap, so they paid cash for both, then hauled the house over in pieces. "Spent the next six months just trying to make it livable," Wink said. "It had no insides. No sinks, no flooring. It was just a shell."

The deck, the plumbing, the siding, the yard: The whole place was a kind of sweat-equity jigsaw puzzle. Even the rock driveway was a bit of luck. "I wanted to use rock to keep it retro," Wink said. The frenzy of construction all over town had provided it for free. To avoid hauling excess rock from building sites to the local landfill, where they paid by the ton, contractors would instead dump their rock in secluded lots all over town. "They'd find a side street like this and just dump a pile of clean, fresh rock," Wink said. "We took that trailer over there, filled it to the rail about fifty times, and brought all of it here."

"There's still a lot of work needs to be done," Sarah said. The wood ties that framed the landscaping were old (they were thinking about replacing them with concrete curbing); the gravel that had scattered and dissipated over the years needed to be filled in (Wink knew where to get some cheap); the deck needed to be replaced.

Had they borrowed against the house? Were they underwater? People approached them, Wink said, "but frankly, the way the value was shooting up so fast kinda scared me. So we just sat tight and watched it all go down around us."

Among the houses we could see—a few up the street, another on the far side of the canal—nearly every one was empty, with some misfortune attached. Sarah shared their legends: a husband in construction, now out of work; a wife in real estate in a dead market; an investor spread too thin; a poor fool hobbled by a DUI.

"We're surviving it," Wink said.

Was it lonely out here?

No, they liked the peace and quiet. Wink ran his hand across the horizon. "Nothing was here when we got here," he said. "We killed I don't know how many rattlesnakes. I'd watch 'em going across that tall grass—just surfin' on it. We got all kinds of foxes and panthers all creeping around here, especially over across the street."

But things weren't so bad, considering.

"In Michigan," Sarah reminded me. "It's *bad.*"

"Worse," I said. "The weather's awful."

"Right!" Wink said, as if he'd long argued this point. "You're not freezing to death. Down here you can be a bum and practically *live.* I mean, if you say you can't eat in Florida, there must be something wrong with you. When I was a kid, we had the mango trees, the orange trees, tangerine, any kind of fruit tree. You've got fish. Every night, I got rabbits and quail coming right to my fence. I got a good, high-powered pellet gun. I could knock a couple off. But Sarah ain't good for that; when we go fishing she's *throwing* bait."

Even on my parents' lot, Wink said, there was enough to harvest and make a little scratch. To prove his point, he led me back across the street. We high-stepped across the grass, across the sand. I dodged a toad, lizards scattered. Wink led me up to a spiky cluster of saw palmettos where, once he'd lifted a pointed frond, I could see a cluster of red berries.

"Every once in a while you see the Mexicans," Wink said. "They'll be over here picking these palmetto berries. They use them berries for prostate cancer. The Seminole Indians used to eat 'em. They got the lowest rate of prostate cancer, and it all come back to the fact that they were eating berries off the saw palmettos like this little clump right here." He plucked one off, held it up, then dropped it in the palm of my hand. "So the Mexicans come and load 'em up in fifty-gallon burlap sacks, then go to the laboratory in LaBelle and sell 'em." He reached down and picked another. "But if you want 'em good, just go straight to the plant."

The trick to it, he said, was to whack the palmettos with a stick first, to rouse and scatter whatever rattlesnakes had nested underneath the fronds. "Shake 'em loose." And as he crept around, stooping and jabbing a stick into the brush, he pointed out other little crops—berries and roots and all kinds of cure-alls and subtle sustenance. Then he tilted his head toward the canal. "You've heard of tilapia, right? I've caught 'em right out of that canal. About this big," he said, spreading his hands.

I looked down at the canal. Waterbugs skimmed the muck.

"High dollar, too," he said.

We shuffled back toward the street. Wink kicked at a tough, black blob. "Looks like tar," he said. At the corner, he pointed out the scourge of the neighborhood—the scourge of Florida, for that matter—the Brazilian Pepper Tree. It, too, produced berries, but a variety that was a delicacy for crows, which gathered in black whorls in the branches to pick the tree clean, with freaky, ravenous thoroughness—getting drunk on the berries all the while. "You'll see a bunch of 'em, and they'll be making a *racket*," Wink said, with a smile to the side of his mouth. "They scream and yell like frat boys. Then they fly off all crooked, like a big party."

And there, next to the Brazilian Pepper, was Wink's favorite plant, a young kapok tree—tall and spiked with horrific-looking thorns, thick as screws, that ran base-to-tip along the thin trunk. Wink knew it as "Thomas Edison's laboratory plant," named for the inventor who spent his winters in Fort Myers, where, on an estate he shared with Henry Ford, he imported and cross-bred thousands of plants in search of a cheap source of rubber, creating an Edenic arboretum, which was now a botanical garden for tourists. Most likely the kapok's seeds had been carried over by a wheeling gull. Wink got a nostalgic kick from the kapok, since it was the same plant he and other kids would lop and trim and use to beat each other, in play or fights, a use which led to its more common name and, according to Wink, the birth of a phrase—the Ugly Stick. He used it plenty when he was young, and smiled talking about it now.

I looked back at the lot. I suppose I should have known better than to assume it was a total loss. Certainly a few saw palmettos weren't going to rescue that forty thousand, but there was now, at least, a scrubby wonder to it.

Walking back to the truck, I marveled once more at the *agave* cactus, like a giant green star that had crashed into the dirt, its thorny sword-shaped leaves fanning out, the middle leaf reaching just above Wink's head. This cactus had been occasion for yet another encounter with the Mexicans, when a handful of them— county workers, apparently, judging by the county truck— happened to spot it one afternoon while working across the street. With shovels in hand, they walked over and surrounded it, resting on their shovels as they pointed and talked. Wink watched them from his window a while, then walked outside. They asked if it was for sale. It was not for sale, he said. They walked away. A couple of nights later, the Mexicans returned—a different truck this time, but with a rope, one end of which they tied to the hitch, with the other lassoed around the cactus. The truck peeled off, the *agave* heaved, the rope snapped. The truck paused just a moment before peeling out again. Wink made it to his window in time to see it whip around the corner and out of sight. He went downstairs to observe the damage, loosened the rope from around his tilted cactus, rather proud of it. After that, he said, the Mexicans gave up.

Sarah pointed to a group of seedlings tucked close to the *agave*. "Little babies," she called them. She liked to plant them around the yard whenever she could.

"You're welcome to have one of 'em if you want," Wink said.

I demurred, but Sarah insisted, then darted inside the house to soak a napkin. She emerged with the napkin and a spade and a plastic bag, kneeled next to the *agave*, and began to dig a seedling out. She wrapped it carefully in the napkin, then lowered it into the bag and cinched the bag shut. I looked at the size of what had spawned this gift, this green, spiked behemoth. I had no idea where to put it. I didn't have the space. My father's yard, maybe, which was big enough, but homogenous, where a plant that looked like a barbed flail would certainly be considered an invasion. The trick would be to plant it without telling him, somewhere in the back, and let it claim its corner, a token of his investment.

I thanked them. I didn't know when I'd be back this way.

"We'll be all right," Wink said. "We're sticking around till the end." All I had to do was swing by. "Come on back, look me up anytime," he said. "Maybe we'll make good friends."

I got in the truck, set the cactus down gently in the seat next to mine. Then I cranked the motor, threw the shift, and pulled away, waving as I crept down the road toward the gentle hum of town.

NOTES

This book could not have been written without the real estate professionals, historians, economists, reporters, and others whose insights helped dissect the complexities of the housing boom and bust, and whose insights also revealed a mystery and depth to Florida I'd failed to appreciate before. I hope the following endnotes give credit where it is due. I hope they'll also provide good leads for writers who wish to pick up the thread of the Florida Story.

SPRING: THE ROUT

My research was led by two books, both of which I returned to again and again. One was Gary Mormino's *Land of Sunshine, State of Dreams: A Social History of Modern Florida* (Gainesville: University Press of Florida, 2005). Professor Mormino also provided an invaluable history lesson through several conversations. I am deeply indebted to him for his generosity. The other book at the top of my Florida canon is Michael Grunwald's *The Swamp: The Everglades, Florida, and the Politics of Paradise* (New York: Simon & Schuster, 2006). Grunwald has written a riveting epic of Florida's ecology and the politics that both cooperated with and competed against it. Any serious conversation about Florida's history and future begins with these two books.

Numerous articles helped provide a framework for how the housing bubble expanded and finally burst. The larger picture of housing policy in America is told in Alyssa Katz's excellent, authoritative work, *Our Lot: How Real Estate Came to Own Us* (New York: Bloomsbury, 2009). I relied on dozens of articles and policy papers to help assemble a brief snapshot of the subprime market and its impact on housing in America; but more importantly, I found a way to make sense of so much mind-numbing research by following the example of Adam Davidson and Alex Blumberg, whose award-winning radio documentary "The Giant Pool of Money" (*This American Life*, Program #355, May 9, 2008) is, hands-down, the best synopsis of how we got into this mess. Not only do they dissect the dizzyingly complex economics of this disaster, they were one of the first media organizations to humanize it, unforgettably so. To piece together what was happening on the ground in Tampa, and how foreclosures were affecting the local real estate market, I relied on my father's accounts as well as information Mena provided. Joe Koebel also provided a great deal of background on the real estate landscape between 2004 and 2008, as did Chuck Collova. Daren Blomquist at RealtyTrac provided the data.

As for the history of Tampa and its various neighborhoods, Henry Plant's history and impact on Tampa was gathered through the Henry B. Plant Museum as well as Kelly Reynolds's biography, *Henry Plant: Pioneer Empire Builder* (Cocoa, Fla.: Florida Historical Society Press, 2003). The museum also possesses a trove of resources that detail the soldiers' experiences in Tampa during the Spanish American War. Susan Braden's *The Architecture of Leisure: The Florida Resort Hotels of Henry Plant and Henry Flagler* (Gainesville: University Press of Florida, 2002) was also extremely rich in detail about the hotel culture of Florida in the nineteenth century.

There are numerous accounts of the beauty and difficulty experienced in early Florida. Books and sources that were especially helpful in revisiting this setting were *Chronicle of the Narváez Expedition* by

Alvar Núñez Cabeza de Vaca (New York: Penguin Books, 2002), William Bartran's *Travels* (New York: Dover, 1955), John McPhee's *Oranges* (New York: Farrar, Straus and Giroux, 1966), *Florida: Land of Change* by Kathryn Abbey Hanna (Chapel Hill: University Press of North Carolina, 1948), and the classic *The Everglades: River of Grass* by Marjory Stoneman Douglas (Sarasota: Pineapple Press, 1997).

Among the numerous nineteenth-century travel guides, I found two facsimiles to be especially useful: Daniel Garrison Brinton's *A Guide-Book to Florida and the South, for Tourists, Invalids and Emigrants* (Gainesville: University Press of Florida, 1978) and *Guide to Florida* by "Rambler" (Gainesville: University Press of Florida, 1964). Articles from the *New York Times*, the New York *Herald*, and New Zealand's *Evening Post* also helped compose a portrait of a place. Jim Schnur of the Special Collections Department at the University of South Florida was extremely helpful in juxtaposing contemporary Tampa Bay with the area explored by the Spanish, and all the layers of development in between.

THE DREAM REVISITED

I would have liked to have discovered Le Corbusier's observation on the "pure joy of geometry" through his own writings, but I'm happy to give credit to Alain de Botton for including it in his brilliant meditation, *The Architecture of Happiness* (New York: Vintage International, 2006).

By now the collapse of Lehman Brothers and the unraveling of the global market it triggered in the fall of 2008 has been widely dissected and explained. Anyone fixated on the subject would have noticed a growing confidence in comparing this crisis with the Great Depression. That comparison evolved from economists aligning the minutiae of both crises to pundits following their lead. The presidential candidates invoked the comparison liberally (Reuters 10/8/08). But when Barack Obama made the comparison during his first press conference as president, on February 8, 2009, with all the authority, deliberateness, and sobriety the office demands, and with nearly every phrase analyzed, the comparison assumed a new gravitas.

The field asset services industry is one that will continue to grow as long as foreclosures remain at crippling levels. Whether companies like FAS and Safeguard and Pacific Preservation Services can operate efficiently enough to move the inventory along, so that homes can be put back into the market in a timely manner, remains doubtful. These companies tackle the overwhelming paperwork that comes with the processing of foreclosures, but coordinating the cleaning out and repair of foreclosures is an altogether different challenge. On an optimistic note, some of these companies have acquired the ability to assume more responsibility over foreclosure management, covering overdue utilities (a huge relief to agents who are already stretched thin).

The ghost subdivision, whether complete or interrupted, provided the iconic stamp of the crisis. There are blogs dedicated to them, and at least one blog I came across dedicated to the variety of shapes they assume when observed via satellite. The Harris family's predicament in Tanglewood Preserve was documented first in the *Tampa Tribune* (August 9, 2008), then the *St. Petersburg Times* (November 17, 2008), and then, most famously, by George Packer in *The New Yorker* (issues of February 9 and 16, 2009).

OPPORTUNITY KNOCKS

Reporting that informed the snapshot of foreclosure resistance is James Barron and Russ Buettner, "Scorn Trails A.I.G. Executives, Even in Their Driveways," the *New York Times* (March 20, 2009); Marcy Kaptur, "Disapproval of Obligations Under the Emergency Economic Stabilization Act of 2008" (www.kaptur.house.gov); Derek Kravitz, "Ex-Owners Turning Aggressive in Efforts to Resist Leaving," the *Washington Post* (May 3, 2009); Michael M. Phillips, "He's Taking Law into His Own Hands to Help Broke Homeowners," the *Wall Street Journal* (June 6, 2008); John Leland, "Sheriff in Chicago Ends Evictions in Foreclosures," the *New York Times* (October 9, 2008); Tom Ramstack, "Sheriff vs. Mortgage Banker," the *Washington Times* (November 24, 2008); Shannon Behnken, "Who Owns Your Loan? It's Time to Find Out," the *Tampa Tribune* (November 17, 2008); and Ben Ehrenreich, "Foreclosure Fightback," *The Nation* (January 22, 2009).

"House of Lies," a series of articles that ran in the *Miami Herald* in 2007, is a startling investigation of the corruption and dysfunction that make a mockery of the city's public-housing system. Beginning in 2008, the *Herald*'s Monica Hatcher continued the investigation with what is, collectively, a definitive portrait of the corruption that fueled Miami's boom and led to its bust. In addition, Jeremy Glazer, of Dade County Commissioner Katherine Sorenson's office, provided excellent insight into the challenges that face housing reform in Miami, as did Arden Shank of Neighborhood Housing Services.

Underwater mortgage statistics were provided by First American CoreLogic.

I assembled the narrative of Take Back the Land not only through my interviews with Max Rameau but through a number of articles and interviews found elsewhere, nearly all of which are archived on their Web site (www.takebacktheland.net). Many articles about similar forms of resistance are archived on their blog (http://takebacktheland .blogspot.com). The *New York Times* front-page story on the Trody family ran on April 9, 2009 (John Leland, "With Advocates' Help, Squatters Call Foreclosures Home"). Police Chief John Timoney's comment on the Trody family was given during his interview with *ABC World News* (April 12, 2009).

Bank walkaways were documented by Susan Saulny, "In Home-owners' Latest Woe, Banks Are Skipping Foreclosures," the *New York Times* (March 30, 2000), and Sandra Livingston, "'Walkaways' by Banks Leave Housing Mess," *Plain Dealer* (July 19, 2009).

Miami's foreclosure numbers were provided by RealtyTrac.

Statistics on underwater mortgages were provided by Carolyn Kemp of the Mortgage Bankers Association.

PAPER BARONS

There are many good books on the history of Miami Beach, but Howard Kleinberg's *Miami Beach: A History* (Miami: Centennial Press, 1994) sets the bar. The story of the island's hotel wars in the 1950s can be found in Steven Gaines's *Fool's Paradise: Players, Poseurs, and the Culture of Excess in South Beach* (New York: Crown, 2009). Further reading on Morris Lapidus and the Fontainebleau includes Martin Mayer, "The Man Who Put Rhinestones on Miami," *Harper's* (March 1965) and Norman Mailer, "Miami and Chicago," *Harper's* (November 1968). Other details of Fisher and the beach's history were drawn from Jane Fisher's *Fabulous Hoosier: A Story of American Achievement* (New York: Robert M. McBride & Co., 1947); and Mark S. Foster's *Castles in the Sand: The Life and Times of Carl Graham Fisher* (Gainesville: University Press of Florida, 2000).

Susan Orlean's *The Orchid Thief: A True Story of Love and Obsession* (New York, Random House, 1998) is a masterpiece of narrative journalism, both for its prose and its blend of contemporary Florida with history. The real estate chicanery that distinguished Lee County in the 1950s is vividly rendered in this book and inspired my own snooping.

David E. Dodrill's *Selling the Dream: The Gulf American Corporation and the Building of Cape Coral, Florida* (Tuscaloosa: University of Alabama Press, 1993) is a wild history of the Rosen brothers and their real estate schemes, and provides a detailed look into Lee County's beginnings and its evolution into the postwar pension sand trap that made Florida infamous once again. A treasure of images of Lehigh Acres and nearby cities can be found in *Lee County: A Pictorial History* by Prudy Taylor Board and Patricia Pope Bartlett (Norfolk, Va.: Donning Co., 1985).

The rest of Lehigh Acres's history comes from the materials my father kept from his visit in 1969, as well as from interviews with Gerald Gould and Rick Anglickis, neither of whom I would have thought to track down had it not been for Kris Hundley's article, "Lehigh Acres: Florida's Lesson in Unregulated Growth," *St. Petersburg Times* (August 9, 2009).

ACKNOWLEDGMENTS

In 1998, after two years of roundtable discussions on the art of fiction at the University of Florida, I left Gainesville with a degree and a good reading list, but not much improvement in mastering the art. My employability hadn't improved all that much, and I really didn't have a clue what to do next, other than keep writing, which I did under my mother's and father's respective roofs. They endured much confusion over what, exactly, I'd been studying to become, and how it was supposed to earn me a living. For all the resilience and loyalty and love they showed me during those years of study and struggle, I am forever indebted to them—to my father especially, who let me earn my room and board honorably that year by working for him, introducing me, thereby, to this story. In essence, this book began the morning I jumped into his truck on yet another ride to yet another job. Every ounce of ink and inch of lead I've spent writing about it since is rooted with him.

When it finally came time to tell this story, a decade later, Bill Wasik was kind enough to take an interest, and wasted little time in getting me back home to report it. He applied a deft hand in editing the final story for *Harper's*. Afterward, my agent, Jennifer Carlson, was instrumental in transforming that article into a book. She worked tirelessly to improve the proposal, then battled to find a home for it. She has supported me without reservation along the way. I'm lucky to have her.

In the group effort that a book becomes, and in showing gratitude where it is due, I owe the highest praise to David Patterson, my editor at Holt, who dug into the manuscript with a dedication that's hard to come by. He always had time to discuss a strategy, and was open to any idea, providing, meanwhile, a guidance that kept me on course. His talent is of the highest caliber, and I'm proud to have worked with him.

The group effort grew over time. Michael Donohue was a vital reader. Matt Dellinger showed great wisdom during countless brainstorming sessions, all while hard at work on his own first book, *Interstate 69: The Unfinished History of the Last Great American Highway*. In mentioning it, I hope to make up for some of the time I stole while he could've been writing.

Ted Genoways wrestled patiently, and brilliantly, with a hydra-headed chapter on foreclosures and homelessness to make it work for *Virginia Quarterly Review*. The reporting for that story was supported by The Investigative Fund. To Ted and Esther Kaplan and her team at the Fund, I am deeply grateful.

I am also grateful—profoundly so—to the National Endowment for the Arts. Without their support, this monster would have devoured its creator, then died half-finished.

The expertise of Debbie Hughes, of the Edison & Ford Winter Estates, and Mike Weston, of the Florida Division of Forestry, were critical in getting to know the dynamic flora of this state. Jim Schnur and Professor Gary Mormino, both of the University of South Florida; Abraham Lavender, of the Miami Beach Historical Society; writer Michael Grunwald, of *Time*—these men were all generous with their time and leads and knowledge of history. I would still be lost in the stacks without their guidance. I would have been lost, too, without Joe Koebel, Mena Reyes, Chuck Collova, and Peter Zalewski, all of whom shared their expertise in studying Florida's real estate landscape, piecing together how it evolved and devolved, and where it might be headed. And among those living through that devolution who were kind enough to share their experiences with me, and those who worked the front lines—Hector, Ismael, Joe Logan, Alan Frazier, the homeowners and laborers and landlords who make up the foreclosure ecosystem, who participated in this book—I'm grateful to all of them, to say the least.

As part of his bulletproof fact-checking, Chris Berdik provided an excellent, insightful reading of the manuscript, and with impressive speed. I would be remiss not to mention that in agreeing to fact-check the book, Chris brought all his skills—as a fact-checker, a journalist, and editor—to the table.

I'm also indebted to Marjorie Braman, of Holt, and her assistant, Rachel Bergmann, both of whom led this book across the finish line with great care. With everyone at Holt, this project landed in excellent hands.

Finally, Diane and Porter Brownlee are owed a special thanks for taking Ellen and me in during a very difficult phase, when we were without a home, between parts of the country, broke, and trying to plan a wedding while finishing the book. And to be sure, Ellen finished it as much as I did. She endured a great deal to keep us together despite the demands of a project that asked much more than I'd anticipated. She took a chance and returned with me to Florida, suffered the tempests of the years that followed, and, rather than flee, became my wife. I have praised others for their strength and resilience and compassion, but I have never seen those qualities demonstrated with such dignity and commitment as I have by her.

This book is yours, love. Here's to a happy home.

ABOUT THE AUTHOR

PAUL REYES is the former editor-at-large of the *Oxford American* magazine and currently a contributing editor with *Virginia Quarterly Review*. In addition to those publications, his writing has appeared in *Harper's*, *Slate*, the *Los Angeles Times Book Review*, the *New York Times*, the *Saint Ann's Review*, and the *Mississippi Review*. In 2010, he received a Literature Fellowship from the National Endowment for the Arts. Reyes lives in Tampa, Florida.